3/99

19.⁹⁵

The Holocaust Remembered Series

The Holocaust Heroes

David K. Fremon

Enslow Publishers, Inc.

44 Fadem Road	PO Box 38
Box 699	Aldershot
Springfield, NJ 07081	Hants GU12 6BP
USA	UK

To Grandpa

Library of Congress Cataloging-in-Publication Data

Fremon, David K.
    The Holocaust Heroes / David K. Fremon.
        p. cm. — (The Holocaust remembered series)
    Includes bibliographical references.
    Summary: Details the efforts of people who risked their own lives to save thousands of Jews and others from Nazi persecution.
    ISBN 0-7660-1046-5
    1. World War, 1939–1945—Jews—Rescue—Juvenile literature.
2. Righteous Gentiles in the Holocaust—Anecdotes—Juvenile literature. 3. World War, 1939–1945—Jewish resistance—Juvenile literature. [1. World War, 1939–1945—Jews—Rescue. 2. Righteous Gentiles in the Holocaust. 3. World War, 1939-1945—Jewish resistance. 4. Holocaust, Jewish (1939–1945)] I. Title. II. Series.
    D804.6.F74 1998
    791.45′652920693—dc21   97-37639
                                    CIP
                                      AC

Printed in the United States of America

10 9 8 7 6 5 4 3 2 1

Illustration Credits: Ben Meed, Courtesy of USHMM Photo Archives p. 98; Central State Archive of Film, Photo, and Photographic Documents, courtesy of USHMM Photo Archives p. 25; Courtesy of USHMM Photo Archives pp. 6, 16, 19, 27, 46, 53, 55, 59, 62, 65, 76, 78, 81, 92, 111; David K. Fremon pp. 109, 114; Helen Yom Tov Herman, courtesy of USHMM Photo Archives p. 69; Library of Congress, courtesy of USHMM Photo Archives p. 12; Main Commission for the Investigation of Nazi War Crimes, courtesy of USHMM Photo Archives pp. 31, 43; Morris Rosen, courtesy of USHMM Photo Archives p. 19; National Archives Collection of World War II War Crime Records, Entry 1, United States Counsel for the Prosecution of Axis Criminality, United States Evidence Files, 1945–46, PS-1061 (STROOP REPORT) pp. 87, 105; National Archives, courtesy of USHMM Photo Archives pp. 5, 9, 49, 105; Peter Feigl, courtesy of the United States Holocaust Memorial Museum p. 46; Professor Leopold Pfefferberg-Page, courtesy of USHMM Photo Archives p. 40; Recreated by Enslow Publishers, Inc. p. 36; Rijksinstituut voor Oorlogsdocumentatie, courtesy of USHMM Photo Archives pp. 69, 95; Thomas Veres, courtesy of USHMM Photo Archives p. 59; Yad Vashem Photo Archives, courtesy of USHMM Photo Archives p. 84; Yelena Brusilovsky, courtesy of USHMM Photo Archives p. 23.

Cover Illustration: Julia Pirotte, courtesy of United States Holocaust Memorial Museum (USHMM) Photo Archives.
Cover Caption: Jewish partisans in action during the August 1944 insurrection in the south of France.

Contents

1

It Would Have Been the End

Silent night, holy night, All is calm, all is bright. . . . On Christmas Eve, 1942, a corner building in the city of Nice in southern France seemed to reflect the serenity of the beloved Christmas carol. Suddenly, the clop-clop-clop of boots broke the silence. Soldiers had entered the building's side door. Ever alert, Kate Rossi heard the noise. The seventeen-year-old French girl woke the three children in her care. They hurried out the front door and ran to the Catholic church across the street. "We didn't take chances," Kate said later. "If they had spotted the boys, it would have been the end."[1] The four spent the night in the church, giving thanks to God that they had evaded capture to live another day.

The three children with Kate were not Catholic. They were Jews fleeing certain death at the hands of Nazi soldiers during World War II. Their mother had left them with Kate's mother before escaping to Spain. When Kate's mother died suddenly, the teenager took

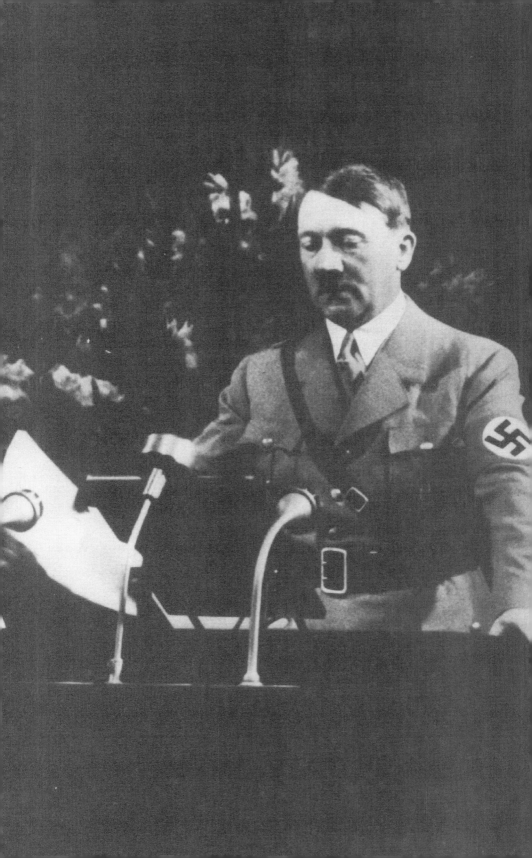

over their care. She called them by Christian names, taught them the rituals of the Catholic Church, and fed and clothed them. Most important, she kept a distance between them and hostile troops.

German dictator Adolf Hitler sought to kill every Jew in Europe, a systematic slaughter known as the Holocaust. Tragically, this mass murder proved highly successful. Some 6 million Jews perished at the hands of the Nazis and their allies—two out of every three Jews in Europe and one third of the Jews in the world.

The total would have been higher if not for the Kate Rossis of Europe. During World War II there were four types of people in Europe: First, there were people who fought and worked to eliminate Jews and "undesirables" from the earth. Then, there were victims, innocent people whose only "crime" was their religion, sexual orientation, or political belief. There were also bystanders, which included most people. They did not actively participate in Nazi atrocities, yet they did nothing to prevent them. By their inaction, they permitted the horrors to continue. However, like Kate Rossi, thousands of others did what they could to save one or more Jews from death. Usually, these efforts came at the risk of their own lives. They were the heroes.

During World War II, heroism took many forms. Gentiles (non-Jews) hid people in their basements or barns. Others created false identity papers or led refugees to safety. Even some Nazi officers helped save lives by not enforcing all rules or by secretly alerting Jews of

Adolf Hitler addresses a 1933 Nazi party rally. After Hitler assumed power in Germany, he immediately began restricting the rights of Jews.

upcoming trouble. Some people took great pains to record the atrocities they witnessed. Jews fought for their lives by joining partisan (guerrilla) units or rebelling in ghettos or death camps. Some Jews died while resisting the Nazis and saving other Jews.

This is the story of some of those heroes.

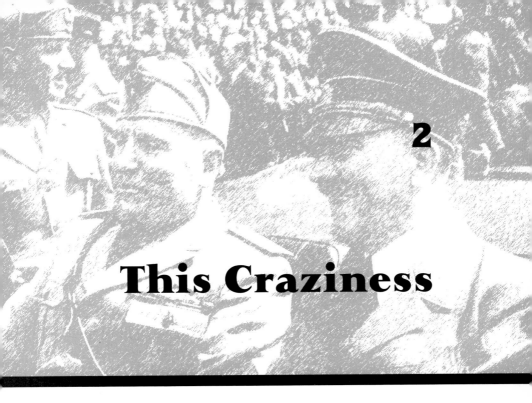

2

This Craziness

Followers of the Jewish religion have lived in Europe for more than two thousand years. Often they were accepted for who they were—pious and hardworking people. Not everyone, however, tolerated his or her Jewish neighbors.

As Christianity grew in Europe, Jews often faced persecution. Many Christian leaders blamed Jews for Jesus' crucifixion, even though pagan Romans were the ones who crucified him. "Christ killer" became a commonly used term for people of the Jewish faith.

Throughout Europe, Christians outnumbered Jews. They generally had more money, and they had more power. As historian Raul Hilberg noted, "The Jews had always been a minority, always in danger, but had learned that they could avert or survive destruction by . . . appeasing their enemies."[1]

When Jews were allowed to live freely, they and their communities prospered. Europe benefited from the wisdom and skills of many Jews, including Dutch philosopher Baruch Spinoza, German composer Felix Mendelssohn, and Austrian psychoanalyst Sigmund Freud.

Jews flourished particularly in Germany. They gained recognition on a worldwide scale. Although the Jews as a group made up less than one percent of Germany's population, they won eleven of thirty-seven Nobel prizes issued to Germans before 1933.

Despite these accomplishments, anti-Semitic (anti-Jewish) discrimination continued. Artists drew Jews as short, fat, unshaved, and big-nosed. "Humorists" pictured them as vultures, vampires, toads, and spiders.

Hundreds of anti-Semitic newspapers existed in Germany during the early 1900s. They accused Jews of raping women, killing children in ritual sacrifices, committing financial robbery, and any other crime imaginable. One such anti-Semitic periodical, *Ostara*, particularly influenced one devoted reader. His name was Adolf Hitler.

Mein Kampf

"When I first met Adolf Hitler, his anti-Semitism was already pronounced," recalled boyhood friend August Kubizek. "And although his experiences in Vienna might have deepened this feeling, they certainly did not give birth to it."[2]

The eighteen-year-old Hitler left his home in Linz in 1907. He hoped to find fame and fortune as an artist in the Austrian capital of Vienna. But once there, he was rejected by an art school. He suffered from depression, and his hatred of the Jews was ever increasing. "Wherever I went, I began to see Jews," Hitler claimed. "I often grew sick to my stomach from [their] smell."[3]

During World War I Hitler fought well for the losing German army. Most historians claim that the Western allies' superior troop and weapon strength defeated the Germans. Hitler blamed the Jews.

After the war, Hitler joined the German Workers' Party (DAP), whose name he later changed to the National Socialist German Workers' Party (NSDAP). Most Germans ignored this party as just another extremist fringe group. But in November 1923, Hitler's followers tried to overthrow Germany's government. This ill-advised Beer Hall *Putsch* earned Hitler a five-year prison term. He was paroled after nine months.

Hitler kept busy while in prison. He started writing *Mein Kampf (My Struggle)*, an autobiography that also laid out his plan for dealing with Germany's "enemies," especially the Jews. The book was published in two volumes, the first appearing in 1925 and the second in 1926. Hitler left no doubt whom he considered Germany's enemies: Communists, liberals, labor unions, and, most of all, Jews.

Hitler Takes Power

Germans were willing to listen to anyone who claimed to have an answer to the nation's ills. After World War I, the country lay in ruins. Germany's postwar government, known as the Weimar Republic, could not control the many extremist political parties that appeared. Victorious allied governments demanded reparations from Germany. To meet these demands, the government was forced to print billions of marks (German currency). Germany's economy had flourished after 1924. But when the depression hit in 1930, the inflated currency became all but worthless.

Hitler, meanwhile, saw his popularity grow. He traveled throughout Germany shouting his venomous speeches. His associate Albert Speer recalled, "For a few short hours the personal unhappiness caused by the breakdown of the economy was replaced by a

Franz Eher Nachf. G. m. b. H.

Deutschvölkische Verlagsbuchhandlung

Fernruf 20047 • München • Thierschstraße 15

Postscheck-Konto: Nr. 11540 München
Bank-Konto: Deutsche Hansabank A.G.,
München

Kommissionär:
Herr Robert Hoffmann, Leipzig

4½ Jahre Kampf
gegen Lüge, Dummheit und Feigheit
Eine Abrechnung von Adolf Hitler

Leitspruch

„Sie müssen sich ge-
genseitig wieder achten
lernen, der Arbeiter der
Stirne den Arbeiter der
Faust und umgekehrt.
Keiner von beiden be-
stünde ohne den ande-
ren. Aus ihnen her-
aus muß sich ein neuer
Mensch kristallisieren:
Der Mensch des kom-
menden Deutschen
Reiches!"

Adolf Hitler.

Der Eher-Verlag kündigt „Mein Kampf" an. 1924

Die kürzere Fassung des endgültigen Titels ist wesentlich schlagkräftiger!

frenzy that demanded victims. . . . By lashing out at their opponents and vilifying the Jews, they gave expression and direction to fierce, primal passions."[4]

At first, such passion did not show itself among German voters. Hitler's party, now known as the National Socialists, or Nazis, won less than 3 percent of the 1928 vote. But as economic conditions further deteriorated, Nazis gained support. In 1930 Nazis received 18 percent of the vote—more than one hundred seats in the Reichstag, the German legislative body.

At the time, aging war hero Paul von Hindenburg led the Weimar Republic as president. He named Hitler chancellor in January 1933. Hindenburg hoped the job's responsibilities would calm the fiery political leader. Instead it fueled his passion.

Less than a month after Hitler became chancellor, a mysterious fire destroyed the Reichstag building. Hitler blamed Communists for the blaze. He used the fire as an excuse to pass the Enabling Law, which abolished parliamentary rule. This law gave him unlimited power.

"The Greatest Cowardice"

Hitler's first months in office were a whirlwind of destructive activity. On April 1, Hitler and the Nazis called for a nationwide boycott of Jewish businesses. These calls met with little protest. Noted German rabbi Leo Baeck commented, "The universities were silent; the courts were silent; the president of the Reich, who had taken the oath on the Constitution, was silent." Baeck called it, "the greatest cowardice. Without that

An early advertisement for Adolf Hitler's autobiography Mein Kampf, *which he wrote while serving a prison sentence for his role in an unsuccessful attempt to overthrow the German government.*

cowardice, all that followed would not have happened."[5]

Seeing that he could move without opposition, Hitler took other actions. By the end of his first year as chancellor, he had completely taken over Germany's government. He destroyed opposition political parties, eliminated state governments, prohibited labor unions, outlawed anti-Nazi assemblies, and set up concentration camps in Germany to imprison his enemies. Jews, in particular, felt his wrath. A series of laws barred them from most professions, removed them from universities, and forced them to sell their businesses. Later, Jews would be forced to wear a yellow six-pointed star on their clothing so that they could easily be identified.

American comedian Harpo Marx had a speaking engagement in the Soviet Union in late 1933. At first he had decided to take a leisurely trip through Germany before going to Moscow. He soon changed his mind. He wrote:

> In Hamburg I saw the most frightening and depressing sight I had ever seen—a row of stores with Stars of David and the word 'Jude' painted on them, and inside, behind half-empty counters, people in a daze, cringing like they didn't know what had hit them and didn't know where the next blow would come from. Hitler had been in power only six months, and his boycott was already in full effect. . . . I got across Germany as fast as I could go.[6]

"They Came for the Jews"

Harpo Marx was not the only person who fled Germany. Holocaust survivor Eva Shane recalled, "My father took us out of Germany, to Belgium, in 1933. He

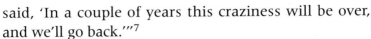

said, 'In a couple of years this craziness will be over, and we'll go back.'"[7]

The craziness did not end. In fact, it got much worse. In 1935 the Nuremberg Laws took away Jews' German citizenship. Aryans (Christian Germans) were forbidden to marry Jews or have sexual relations with them. The laws defined Jews as being of a race, not a religion. Anyone—even practicing Christians—with three Jewish grandparents was considered a full Jew. Eventually, even those with only one Jewish grandparent were considered Jewish and denied their rights as German citizens.

More than four hundred laws were passed between 1933 and 1939 that targeted Jews. These laws either forced Jews to engage in humiliating activities or barred them from doing useful ones. In August 1938, male Jews were required to use the middle name Israel, and female Jews were required to call themselves Sarah. Children's lives changed as they became outcasts. They were forbidden to attend school or go to libraries, movies, and parks. German schools taught children that Jews were inferior and a danger to other German people. Jews were required to register their businesses with the government. By 1938, they were required to turn over those businesses to Aryan Germans.

Jews were not the only victims of discrimination. Nazis arrested others as well and crowded the concentration camps with Communists and other political opponents, homosexuals, and Gypsies. Jehovah's Witnesses, members of a small religious group who refused to accept military service, also went to the camps.

Isolated voices spoke out against the Nazi terrors. They also criticized those who did nothing to stop them. German pastor Martin Niemöller wrote,

Even children were forced to wear the six-pointed star identifying them as Jews.

First they came for the communists, and I did not speak out—because I was not a communist. Then they came for the trade unionists, and I did not speak out—because I was not a trade unionist. Then they came for the Jews, and I did not speak out—because I was not a Jew. Then they came for me—and there was no one left to speak out for me.[8]

Kristallnacht

Herschel Grynszpan waited nervously in the German embassy of Paris. The seventeen-year-old Jewish student raged that Nazis had deported his parents from Germany to Poland. He sought revenge.

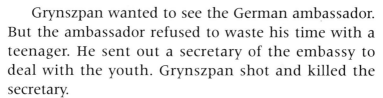

Grynszpan wanted to see the German ambassador. But the ambassador refused to waste his time with a teenager. He sent out a secretary of the embassy to deal with the youth. Grynszpan shot and killed the secretary.

Normally, the murder of a minor government official does not cause massive retaliation. But for Hitler and the Nazis in November 1938, it created the excuse they needed. The killing led to a nationwide night of violence against Jews throughout Germany.

Early in November, Gestapo chief Heinrich Müller sent a telegram to his units that read, "In shortest order, actions against Jews and especially their synagogues will take place in all Germany. These are not to be interfered with."[9]

The assaults took place on November 9. Nazis set fire to more than a thousand German synagogues. They rampaged through cities, destroying more than seven thousand Jewish businesses. Broken glass from this controlled riot gave it the name *Kristallnacht* ("Night of the Broken Glass"). More than property was destroyed. Over two hundred Jews were killed. Thirty thousand more were arrested and sent to concentration camps.

Germans added insult to injury. The government charged that Kristallnacht was the fault of the Jews. Insurance money that should have gone to Jewish victims instead went to the Nazi government. Furthermore, the government demanded a one-billion-mark ($400-million) penalty from the Jewish community.

Nazi leaders called Kristallnacht a "spontaneous" action against Jews. Most people knew otherwise. A Nazi party report to Gestapo commander Hermann Göring said, "Down to the last man, the public knows that political actions like that of 9th November are organized and carried out by the Party, whether this is admitted or not."[10]

Many Jews recognized that it was not safe for them to remain in Germany. They would do anything possible to escape this danger-filled land.

Emigration

About 150,000 Jews fled from Germany during the first two years of Hitler's rule. Another 150,000 left in the months following Kristallnacht. Many more tried to leave. The government, which had already stripped them of their wealth, demanded the equivalent of $200 apiece (or $1,000 per family) for exit visas.

Hundreds of Jews, including prominent intellectuals, left the country. These included conductor Otto Klemperer, film director Fritz Lang, and playwright Bertolt Brecht. Hitler might have denounced "Jew scientists," but the United States was happy to welcome physicist Albert Einstein.

For most Jews, there was no welcome mat. Some foreign nations simply refused to accept Jewish refugees. Others, including the United States, imposed rigid entry requirements. The United States government used the excuse that it could not absorb new workers. Even a bill that would allow entry to refugee children did not pass in Congress.

Herschel Grynszpan's (top) assassination of a minor government official in revenge for his parents' deportation was used by the Nazis as an excuse to unleash a nationwide night of violence against Jews throughout Germany. The synagogue in Ober Ramstadt (bottom) was among hundreds that burned during Kristallnacht. Firefighters made sure that nearby homes were unharmed but did nothing to save the synagogue.

Representatives from thirty-two nations met in July of 1938 in Évian, France. United States president Franklin D. Roosevelt organized the conference, hoping that other nations would admit refugee Jews. Conference delegates discussed problems of refugees without mentioning the Jews. They discussed sending refugees to remote areas like the Philippine Islands, the offshore African island of Madagascar, or near the Orinoco River in Venezuela. One country, the Dominican Republic, agreed to accept one hundred thousand refugees. No other nation made any commitments.

Even a visa to a foreign land was no guarantee for Jews. On May 13, 1939, the S.S. *St. Louis* set sail for Havana, Cuba. Its 936 passengers (all but six were Jews) held Cuban landing permits. "The whole atmosphere on the boat was one of joy and elation," recalled passenger Hans Fischer.[11] However, a shock awaited them in Havana. Cuban officials, for reasons never explained, had invalidated the permits.

The *St. Louis*'s captain then sailed toward Miami, hoping for American support. He found none. Frustrated passengers saw the bright lights of the Florida city. They also saw American Coast Guard boats ready to capture any ship-jumpers. After a few days, the captain gave up and sailed back to Europe.

Of the refugees, 288 found safety in England. The rest ended up in Nazi-occupied France, Belgium, or the Netherlands. Most of those refugees thought the *St. Louis* would be a one-way ticket to freedom. Instead, it was a round-trip to doom.

Germany Goes to War

Hitler's terrorism extended beyond Germany's borders. He sought a European empire that would be ruled by Germans and free of Jews. Nazi forces marched into Austria in early 1938. Austrians welcomed the

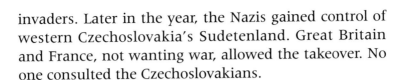

invaders. Later in the year, the Nazis gained control of western Czechoslovakia's Sudetenland. Great Britain and France, not wanting war, allowed the takeover. No one consulted the Czechoslovakians.

Foreign conquests only sharpened Hitler's hatred of the Jews. Hitler declared in 1939 that if Jews succeeded in plunging Germany into war, it would be the end of the Jewish people. The Jews had no intention of starting a war. Hitler had no intention of avoiding one.

Germany attacked Poland on September 1, 1939. Polish troops held out for nearly a month. The Nazis finally conquered their eastern neighbor and began a reign of terror. Within nine months, Denmark, Norway, and most of Western Europe would also fall. In 1941, Hitler broke a peace treaty with the Soviet Union. Thousands of German troops marched to attack the giant Eastern nation.

The Final Solution

With most of Europe under his control, Hitler could concentrate on eliminating Jews. This mass destruction has come to be called the Holocaust, from a Greek word meaning "sacrifice totally burned by fire."

Top SS (Gestapo) officials met in the Berlin suburb of Wannsee in January 1942. By most accounts, the participants enjoyed the gathering. Their topic, however, was anything but friendly. They left no documents of the conference and used code words to hide their real intentions. "Resettlement in the East" meant transportation to death camps. The "Final Solution" was death for all Jews.

Even before Wannsee, mass extermination of Jews had begun. Special troops, the *Einsatzgruppen*, went with the regular German soldiers as they invaded countries. From the Baltic Sea in the north to the Black Sea in the south, these trained killing squads had only one mission. They rounded up Jews and other declared enemies, gathered their valuables, took them outside of town, shot them, and quickly buried their bodies.

In one instance, *Einsatzgruppen* murdered thirty-three thousand people in a two-day period at Babi Yar near the Ukrainian city of Kiev. Overall, they killed nearly a quarter of the Jews who died during the Holocaust. Anti-Jewish residents of Lithuania, Latvia, Belorussia, Russia, and the Ukraine willingly helped with the executions.

But the mobile killing squads took a lot of time and ammunition. Also, many of the men, upset by their constant murdering of people, became alcoholics. Nazi leaders sought a more efficient and less personal method of mass killing.

Belgian Anne Somerhausen recalled hearing of Jews' being shipped in cars and killed with poison gas along the way. "It is a ridiculous story, of course," she commented in her diary. "Who would believe these fantastic tales about gassing people?"[12] The "fantastic tales" were true. Nazis were using gas vans to exterminate victims.

Then they discovered a method even more vile than the killing vans. Zyklon B (hydrogen cyanide) is a poisonous gas. When a pellet was dropped into a chamber, it would turn to gas almost immediately. This gas suffocated the people inside in three to fifteen minutes. Large numbers of Jews were placed in rooms where the gas was released and died almost instantly.

Three-year-old Anna Glinberg's short life was snuffed out at the mass execution at Babi Yar.

Hundreds of concentration camps already existed in Germany and the rest of Europe. These camps served mainly to hold political prisoners. Then the Nazis began building a new type of camp in Poland. Six camps—Auschwitz, Sobibór, Treblinka, Belzec, Chelmno, and Maidanek—had sections where prisoners performed slave labor. But their main purpose was death. Jews were killed in gas chambers disguised as shower rooms. Then their bodies were cremated. Thick clouds of smoke rising from crematorium smokestacks gave a constant death signal. At its peak, Auschwitz killed thirty-four thousand people every twenty-four hours.

Hundreds of trains took passengers on one-way trips to these camps. Jews were forced to pay for their "resettlement." Thousands, loaded into cattle cars, did not even survive the journey. They perished from hunger, thirst, overcrowding, or freezing.

Arbeit macht frei (Work makes one free) declared the sign that hung over the Auschwitz entrance. One commander was more honest. He told new arrivals, "Forget your wives, children, and families; here you will die like dogs."[13]

By 1942, few Jews had any doubts of Nazi plans. Dutch survivor Hedy de Luy commented, "Germans were supposedly shipping people to work in the East. But grandparents and babies were gone. *They* weren't able to work."[14]

Some prisoners escaped immediate execution. Instead, they worked long hours and received inadequate

After conquering Poland, Denmark, Norway, and most of Western Europe, the German army began its assault on the Soviet Union (top). A Russian woman (bottom) grieves for her loved ones amid the ruins of her village.

food rations. They literally worked themselves to death while making weapons for the German army.

Even if they were starved and exhausted, Jews had to look ready for work. They needed incredible courage and mental energy to last one more day. They also needed hope that one more day might bring them closer to liberation. "You could never feel sorry for yourself. You could never break down, because that would be the end," said Holocaust survivor Eva Shane.[15]

Those who lived through the death camps bore lifelong scars. Auschwitz survivor Elie Wiesel commented, "Never shall I forget . . . the first night in camp, which has turned my life into one long night. . . . Never shall I forget that smoke. Never shall I forget the brittle faces of the children. . . . Never shall I forget these things, even if I am condemned to live as long as God."[16]

Not every Jew shared Wiesel's experience. Nazis and their followers tried to destroy the Jews. But there were also thousands who dedicated themselves to saving them.

The Right Thing to Do

3

aria von Maltzan answered the loud knocks on her door. Two Gestapo soldiers requested permission to enter the young woman's apartment. Von Maltzan had no choice. Even though she was descended from German nobility, she was now a suspect.

The soldiers had heard rumors that von Maltzan was hiding a Jew. They searched throughout the apartment. One saw a large couch—big enough for a person to hide inside. He questioned her about it.

Hans Hirschel, a Jewish writer who was hiding inside the couch, shuddered. Von Maltzan was not only his rescuer, she was in love with him. Would she be forced to surrender him?

Von Maltzan defied the soldiers. There was no one inside the couch, she told them. If they did not believe her, they could shoot it. "I told them, 'Go ahead, but you'd better be prepared to pay for the repair of my couch.' They didn't. They left."[1]

Hundreds of rescuers faced close calls like von Maltzan's. Some lost such gambles and paid with their lives and the lives of those they sheltered.

Rescuers needed nerves of steel. Often, acting ability helped. "They had the self-confidence to believe they could do what they did," said Holocaust historian Gay Block.[2]

At the same time, they knew their limitations. Most rescuers realized they could not save everybody. They were brave, but not foolhardy. After the Gestapo left, Maria von Maltzan sent Hans Hirschel away for several weeks. The risk would be too great for both of them if he stayed.

Who Were the Rescuers?

Anyone with the opportunity and desire could have been a rescuer. There was no single category of heroes. Doctors, lawyers, students, farmers, teachers, blacksmiths, fishermen, police officers, and retirees—people from all walks of life did what they could to save Jewish lives. Some were rich and some were poor. Some lived in cities, others lived in small towns or in the country. The one quality they shared was compassion. They saw that something wrong was being done, and they tried to right that wrong. Many came from strong moral backgrounds. Their religious or social beliefs taught them to help others.

Yet even the most upright people were sometimes forced to perform acts they would otherwise consider immoral. Marian Pritchard was a Dutch student. One day she saw German soldiers throwing Dutch children onto a truck. The truck would take them to a concentration camp. When two women protested, the Germans threw them onto the truck. From that day, Pritchard vowed to fight Nazi tyranny.

Pritchard hid a family in the basement of a country house. One night, four SS officers and a Dutch Nazi policeman came to search the house, but they did not find the fugitives.

An hour later, the Dutch Nazi returned for a surprise visit. A friend had given her a revolver, but she had never expected to use it. "I had to kill him," Pritchard later said. "I knew I had no other choice, but I still wish there had been some other way."[3]

Friendship or kinship with Jewish people motivated some rescuers. Individual Jews were relatives, neighbors, business partners, or doctors. Some Christians recalled the Jewish roots of their own religion.

Yet, for reasons such as money, even some anti-Semites rescued Jews. Ephraim Shtenkler's father left his eleven-year-old son with a Polish woman. The woman made no secret of her anti-Jewish views. One day she told Ephraim, "I'll drown you in the well this very day."[4] Yet she kept him for more than four years.

Hatred of Nazis spurred many rescuers. For many, their lifesavings were a part of their politics. The *Comite de Defense des Juifs* (Committee for the Defense of the Jews, or CDJ) in Belgium saved more than three thousand Jewish children. Most were placed in Aryan homes and taught Christian customs. The CDJ also provided money, false documents, and hiding places for adults. Rescue efforts became part of the group's political plan. One Belgian remembered,

> There was not a single . . . weak character who did not reconsider ten times before he dared commit an act of treachery or anti-Semitism. They knew . . . that somewhere in the dark there was the patriot who watched. Somewhere in the shadows . . . was a witness to his deed, . . . a patriotic justice which knew of no mercy for traitors.[5]

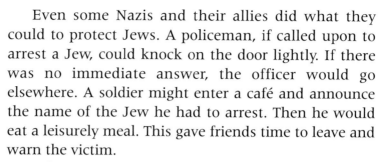

Even some Nazis and their allies did what they could to protect Jews. A policeman, if called upon to arrest a Jew, could knock on the door lightly. If there was no immediate answer, the officer would go elsewhere. A soldier might enter a café and announce the name of the Jew he had to arrest. Then he would eat a leisurely meal. This gave friends time to leave and warn the victim.

Others actively helped Jews. Kurt Loewenthal remembered, "One time we escaped because I happened to know one of the policemen, and he said, 'Don't sleep in your house this night.'"[6] James Loewenson recalled a French policeman who allowed a bus filled with Jews to pass into Switzerland. "This policeman, who had orders to arrest these Jews, let them go free, in plain view of his colleagues. He risked his liberty and his life for us."[7]

Professionals often had opportunities to rescue Jews and devoted their lives to saving others. To them, a rescue was a logical part of their work. Doctors in Denmark became known as *Den Heide Brigade* (the White Brigade). When Nazis ordered a roundup of Danish Jews, the doctors hid the Jews in psychiatric hospitals or nurses' residences.

Families sometimes used children in rescue efforts. They served valuable roles as spies, guides, or message carriers. In case the children were stopped, they were trained to lie convincingly.

What did rescuers do? Anything and everything that was necessary. They fed and clothed their charges and disposed of human wastes. They tried to make a very bad situation as tolerable as possible for the refugees. They had to do these things without attracting attention from the outside world. Refugees, in turn, had to cooperate with their rescuers. They had to stay

Arbeit macht frei *(Work makes one free) was the motto of the Auschwitz camp. However, death, not labor, was the major purpose of Auschwitz and other death camps.*

invisible. If possible, they would help around the house.

Rescuers had to be prepared for any problem. How does someone take care of major illnesses when no doctor can be trusted? How do you dispose of the body of a refugee who died while in your care? The solutions had to be ingenious. When one of Theresa Weerstra's refugees became pregnant, Theresa faked a pregnancy. When the refugee's child arrived, Theresa "gave birth." She pretended the baby was her own. She was then able to get baby supplies without attracting attention.

31

Hiding Jews sometimes took extraordinary nerve. Irene Opdyke, a young Catholic Polish woman, was captured by Germans. They sent her to work in a munitions factory. While there, she befriended twelve Jews who worked in the plant's laundry room. A German major invited her to become his housekeeper. She accepted. Then she smuggled her Jewish friends into the basement of the major's villa. One day, the major came home early and found the Jews. The officer could have had Opdyke and the Jews executed. Instead, he let them stay if Opdyke became his mistress. To save her friends, she agreed. A few months later, they all were able to escape.

Some Jews were easier to hide than others. Blond Jewish females who "looked" Aryan and did not speak with Jewish accents could pass for non-Jews. Males with dark curly hair and heavy accents could not blend in with the general population. Also, all Jewish males were circumcised, but few Gentiles in Europe at the time had received the operation.

Rescue involved more than just hiding Jews. People needed false identification papers, ration cards for food, and money. Forgers kept busy supplying these documents.

Travel for Jews was extremely unsafe. A police officer or soldier could stop anyone at any time. A wrong response might mean death. Some rescuers escorted refugees to havens or border towns. From there, another guide would lead them to safety.

Kate Rossi was one of those guides. Nazis had deported her father to a concentration camp early in the war. From that time, she was a French resistance member. Rossi made ten trips from Nice to Lyon, France, leading refugees to safety. "Every time, it was to a different dropoff place, by a different route," she said. "I always claimed I was going to visit my grandmother."[8]

Sometimes, the conditions became difficult. Once she accompanied a boy who spoke with a thick Jewish accent. They solved that problem by pretending he was a deaf-mute. While she was traveling, her mother cared for three Jewish children. When her mother died, Rossi stopped traveling and took over the children's care.

Not all guides had easy going. Residents of Nieuwlande, Holland, decided to protect Jews. Every home would protect a Jew or Jewish family. The Nazis had ordered that all Jews in Holland were to go to Amsterdam. Arnold Douwes helped rescue about three thousand of those refugees. Often, he had to lie to them. "I'd go to Amsterdam and tell a Jewish family, 'Come with me. I know a wonderful farm where there is plenty of food and you'll be safe,'" he said. "Was there such a place? Of course not! But we'd never have been able to get them out of Amsterdam if we had told them the truth."[9]

Rescue involved many problems. "Imagine how difficult it would be to take children 3 to 6 months old from their parents and not be able to tell the parents where their children would be," said Belgian rescuer Fela Herman.[10]

Young children were unpredictable. Many families tried to pass off Jewish children as Christians. They were given Christian names and taught Christian rituals. But a wrong word, a forgotten name, or an incorrect gesture could be fatal.

Their make-believe lives also damaged the children. Gaby Cohen, a Jewish member of the French resistance, helped hide Jewish children. "The hard task was to convince little children that they were no longer Abraham Levin but Alfred Levoisier, not Sarah Weiss but Suzanne Voison," she said. One boy had his Polish-Jewish name changed to a French-Jewish one, then to a French-Christian one. One day he cried, "Maybe nobody remembers my real name."[11]

If children suffered from psychological dangers, adults posed real ones. "You had to be suspicious of everybody," commented Kate Rossi. "If you didn't get the right number or the right signal, you had to change your plans immediately."[12] One notable traitor was an agent known as La Belle Irene. She took truckloads of Jewish children as if to liberate them. Instead, she turned them over to the Nazis. Hundreds died at her hands.

Aart and Johtje Vos

A Jewish friend asked Dutch resistance members Aart and Johtje Vos to keep a suitcase of valuables until he returned from the ghetto. Then another friend asked to stay overnight. Others followed. "We had 36 people hiding in our house at one time," Aart recalled. "You can't understand what that takes."[13]

It took courage, hard work, and foresight. The Voses dug a tunnel from their house to a forest several hundred yards away. They hid the tunnel under the false bottom of a coal bin in their garden.

They risked their own lives and the lives of their four young children. Were they afraid? "Oh, God, yes!" Johtje exclaimed. "I was scared to death."[14] She added, "We did it because we believed it was the right thing to do."[15]

Miep Gies

Not all rescue attempts ended successfully. The most famous failure took place in Amsterdam.

Otto Frank was a prosperous German businessman. Like many other Jews, he fled soon after Adolf Hitler took power. Later he sent for his wife and daughters,

Margot and Anne. The Franks had enough money to escape to England, but Otto thought they would be safe in the Netherlands.

He was proven wrong. Germans invaded in May 1940. By then, escape routes were blocked. The Franks, like other Jews in the Netherlands, faced discrimination. Otto Frank, however, had prepared for the worst. He sold his business to a partner and quietly prepared a hiding place.

In July 1942, Margot received a letter. She had to report for deportation to Germany. This meant certain death. Wasting no time, the Franks abandoned their home and moved to the hiding place. A business partner, his wife, their son, and a dentist friend joined them in hiding later.

The eight people lived above Otto Frank's office. During the day, they had to remain quiet. At night, they could move about and enter the office.

These refugees needed someone to take care of their needs. Frank had asked bookkeeper Miep Gies to be their link to the outside world. She agreed to help.

Gies, her husband, and a few other employees aided the refugees. They brought food, medicine, books, and news of the outside world. Gies saw them early in the morning to get a list of needed supplies. At lunchtime, her husband and other employees visited, then she returned with the supplies in the afternoon. At the end of the day, someone advised the group when it was safe to move around.

Miep Gies and her husband once spent a night in the Franks' hiding place. They were treated as honored guests. Even so, she recalled, "The fright of these people who were locked up here was so thick I could feel it pressing down on me. . . . For the first time I knew what it was like to be a Jew in hiding."[16] They stayed in hiding for more than two years. Then someone

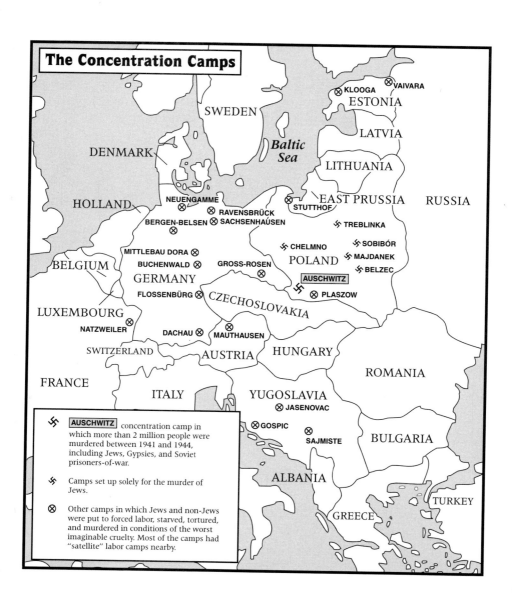

The Concentration Camps

SWEDEN

Baltic Sea

DENMARK

HOLLAND

BELGIUM

LUXEMBOURG

FRANCE

SWITZERLAND

GERMANY

ITALY

ESTONIA

⊗ KLOOGA   ⊗ VAIVARA

LATVIA

LITHUANIA

EAST PRUSSIA   RUSSIA

✡ STUTTHOF

✡ TREBLINKA

✡ CHELMNO   ✡ SOBIBÓR

✡ MAJDANEK

POLAND   ✡ BELZEC

AUSCHWITZ

⊗ PLASZOW

NEUENGAMME ⊗
⊗ RAVENSBRÜCK
BERGEN-BELSEN ⊗ ⊗ SACHSENHAUSEN
⊗

MITTLEBAU DORA ⊗
BUCHENWALD ⊗   GROSS-ROSEN ⊗
FLOSSENBÜRG ⊗   CZECHOSLOVAKIA

NATZWEILER ⊗

DACHAU ⊗ ⊗ MAUTHAUSEN

AUSTRIA   HUNGARY

YUGOSLAVIA
⊗ JASENOVAC

⊗ GOSPIC
⊗ SAJMISTE

ALBANIA

GREECE

ROMANIA

BULGARIA

TURKEY

✡ AUSCHWITZ concentration camp in which more than 2 million people were murdered between 1941 and 1944, including Jews, Gypsies, and Soviet prisoners-of-war.

✡ Camps set up solely for the murder of Jews.

⊗ Other camps in which Jews and non-Jews were put to forced labor, starved, tortured, and murdered in conditions of the worst imaginable cruelty. Most of the camps had "satellite" labor camps nearby.

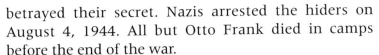

betrayed their secret. Nazis arrested the hiders on August 4, 1944. All but Otto Frank died in camps before the end of the war.

Gies returned to the hiding place soon after the arrests. She recovered Anne Frank's diary, which would become the most famous personal document of the war and the Holocaust.

"I willingly did what I could to help. My husband did too," Gies commented. "It was not enough."[17]

Eva Cohn's Saviors

For every Jew who was saved, there might have been as few as one person or as many as thirty people who helped. Eva Cohn's story was one example of the latter. It involved courage and more than a bit of luck.

Eva's family fled from Germany to Belgium soon after Hitler took power. In 1940, the Nazis invaded Belgium. Eva's father had to report to the new government. They sent him to a camp in Perpignan, France. Twelve-year-old Eva, her mother, and her brother were left alone.

"My father escaped. He raced to a train station. When he saw a train leaving the station, he dashed past a checkpoint before guards could stop him," she said.[18] He got off the train and got a job in Mâcon, France. Then he sent for his family.

They had to get past Nazi border guards to enter France. "Our name—Cohn—was a death sentence. Either you had to go underground—get a *passeur* [a guide]—or get papers. That was impossible for a Jew,"

Germans held prisoners in concentration camps throughout Europe. Six cities in Poland were specially designed as death camps.

Eva Cohn recalled.[19] Eva's mother hired a smuggler to sneak them past the border. But a day before they were scheduled to leave, the smuggler was arrested. Her only hope was to seek mercy from the local police commander. She got it.

Mrs. Cohn told the commander that her husband was a Jew. He had been captured and sent to a camp. Now she was going to stay with a relative in France. She did not say that the relative was her husband. Eva commented, "The commander knew very well what was going on, but he gave us full transit papers anyway."[20] Those papers allowed Eva and her family to reach Mâcon.

Once there, they got new identities. Eva Cohn became Jacqueline Mouton. They were the only Jews in the area. The entire village knew of their plight. The mayor found them a farmhouse outside of town. "People were wonderful. Farmers helped. The next morning we found all kinds of food in front of the door," Eva Cohn recalled.[21]

One day, police took Eva's father's passport. They told him and his family to report to the train station in twenty-four hours. This meant they were to be deported and killed.

There was no place to hide. Jews without papers could be killed instantly. But luck did not abandon the Cohn family. Eva's father told his problem to a Russian friend. They went to another man. Then the three went to the police station. "Give this man his papers," the second man demanded.[22] The police chief returned the passport to Eva's father.

Dozens of their friends and relatives perished in the Holocaust. The Cohn family survived together. "[Jews] could not do it on their own. They had to have help from Gentiles," Eva Cohn said.[23]

Oskar Schindler

Rescuers of Jews were heroes, but not all of them were saints. Oskar Schindler was a gambler, a con artist, a drinker, a womanizer, and a corrupt briber. To more than a thousand Jews, he was also a savior.

Schindler wheeled, dealed, and bribed his way to a fortune. He joined the Nazi party. Schindler never believed in Nazi ideals, especially hatred of the Jews. He joined the party because it provided good business connections.

One day, he saw SS troops herding women and children into a truck. Suddenly, the troops started shooting girls on the street. A young girl in a red coat and hat watched the massacre. The SS murderers ignored the witness. They knew they would kill her sooner or later.

Schindler claimed, "Beyond this day, no thinking person could fail to see what would happen. I was now resolved to do everything in my power to defeat the system."[24]

After Germany took over Poland, Jews were forced from their businesses. Schindler bought one such factory at a cheap price. He inherited forty-five workers. His office manager, a Jew named Itzhak Stern, persuaded him to hire Stern's Jewish friends. Soon the factory had 150 Jewish workers. It produced pots, pans, and mess kits for the German army.

The workers made no money. Their "salaries" went to the German government. However, Schindler promised, "If you work here, you'll live through the war."[25]

Schindler developed a special relationship with "his" Jews. "I knew the people who worked for me," he later explained. "When you know people, you have to behave towards them like human beings."[26]

Schindler had to act friendly to the Nazis while protecting his Jewish workers. Felix Kaminsky recalled,

"Once he had a party for German big shots, and one was drunk and wanted to shoot some Jews. Schindler came to us in the kitchen and said, 'Run away, leave everything, run!' He walked on two sides—for the Germans and for the Jews."[27]

The Jews of Schindler's factory lived in the Plaszow concentration camp. Amon Goeth, a sadist who enjoyed shooting Jews for target practice, ran the camp. Schindler disliked Goeth but made a deal with him. Schindler agreed to use his own money to build a camp for "his" Jews. He spent a fortune to build this camp. Jews there were treated much better than those of Plaszow. By now Schindler's factory had more than seven hundred workers.

Bad news came in 1944. Nazis ordered the Plaszow camp closed. All the camp's Jews—including all Schindler's workers—appeared bound for death camps.

Schindler acted fast. He bought a factory in his native Czechoslovakia. Then he convinced SS officials that his workers were vital to him. No doubt hefty bribes helped persuade the officers. Schindler arranged the transfer of eight hundred men and three hundred women to his factory.

The women's train stopped at Auschwitz. For three terrifying weeks, Schindler's female employees expected death. They overheard an expression at Auschwitz: "You go in through the big doors and you go out through the chimney."[28]

Oskar Schindler poses next to his horse at his enamelware factory in Krakow-Zablocie. By employing mainly Jewish workers, Schindler provided a temporary haven for Jews in Krakow seeking protection from deportation.

Somehow, Schindler rescued them. Details are uncertain, although it appears that large amounts of money changed hands. Every woman except one— Stern's mother—was saved.

Survivor Rena Finder admitted Schindler's flaws. "He enjoyed the wheeling and dealing and doing outrageous things—living on the edge," she said. "But then he realized if he didn't save us, nobody would."[29]

4

Christians Must Not Forget

or years, the Roman Catholic Church had a policy known as sanctuary. A Catholic who was wanted for a crime could enter a church building. Priests or nuns would give that person protection. Government authorities, fearing the power of the Church, would not arrest him or her.

During World War II, many pastors offered such sanctuary. They did what they could to protect refugees, especially Jews. Catholics, Protestants, Orthodox Christians, and members of other faiths helped the rescue effort.

Roman Catholics formed the largest Christian denomination. Officially, the Catholic Church did nothing to protect the Jews. If anything, the Church's indifference encouraged persecution. On July 8, 1933, Pope Pius XI signed a treaty with Nazi Germany. He agreed not to oppose the Nazis. In turn the new government would not disturb Catholic churches. Pius XI later denounced Nazi aggression. But neither he nor his

successor, Pope Pius XII, spoke out publicly against the killing of Jews.

Because of the Church's stand, many church leaders were insensitive to the Jews' plight. Slovakia's Catholic priests, if anything, encouraged the slaughter. But Holland's Catholic bishops forbade Dutch Catholic police from hunting for Jews.

Individual Catholics took action, which saved many lives. Father Angelo Giuseppe Roncalli served as apostolic delegate to Bulgaria, Turkey, and Greece. He helped individual Jews in Slovakia, Hungary, Italy, and France. Chaim Barlas, a representative from a Jewish agency, told Roncalli of problems in Bulgaria. German authorities were pressuring King Boris to deport Bulgaria's Jews.

Roncalli knew the Bulgarian king well. He was the godfather of the king's son. He wrote a letter to Boris, asking him to save Bulgaria's Jews. The king then forbade their deportation.

Some church groups worked openly to stop the Holocaust. The Religious Society of Friends opposed war and injustice. Members, known as Quakers, strove to protect Jews. They provided hiding places, food, clothing, and passage to safety. Quaker service committees in the United States and Great Britain provided funds for Jewish emigration.

Most pastors did not wait for official Church approval. They acted individually. Like other rescuers, they saw injustice against innocent people. It was their duty to help cure that injustice.

André and Magda Trocmé

Magda Trocmé, the wife of Pastor André Trocmé, remembered, "A woman knocked on my door one evening and said she was a German Jew coming from northern France, and that she was in danger. She heard that in Le Chambon somebody could help her. Could she come into my house? I said, 'Naturally, come in.'"[1] That started a rescue effort led by Magda and André. Their town's work saved five thousand Jewish lives.

Centuries earlier, French Catholics had persecuted Protestants. Some Huguenots, as the Protestants were known, escaped to southern France. One group settled in the village of Le Chambon-sur-Lignon. Their descendants knew how it felt to be part of a religious minority. They accepted people of other faiths. Le Chambon residents did not see Jews as vicious Christ killers, as some other Christians did. Instead, they saw religious links between Judaism and Christianity.

Protestant minister André Trocmé hated violence and protested against injustice. When the Nazis conquered France in 1940, they split the country into two regions. The northern region came under direct German control. For the southern half, the Germans established a puppet government in the city of Vichy. They placed World War I hero Henri Philippe Pétain as head of state, but Germany ran the show. Trocmé refused to recognize the puppet government. His school did not fly the Nazi flag or hang Pétain's picture on the walls.

Trocmé set up a network to help the Jews. Members of his church helped. So did Catholics throughout the area. In houses and barns, they sheltered individual Jews and families. Several Jews were smuggled across the Swiss border. Some children were passed off as Christians. No one was turned away from Le Chambon. No one was betrayed.

Youth groups such as Bible study classes and the Boy Scouts were particularly helpful. They relayed messages, such as news about upcoming raids, to hidden Jews. The youth minister of Vichy's puppet government visited Le Chambon. He sought young

people's help in capturing Jews. They refused to cooperate with him.

Refugees there enjoyed some advantages. Le Chambon was a summer tourist resort. Unfamiliar faces did not surprise local residents. Thus a Jew could enter the town and find shelter without arousing attention.

More important, local police were sympathetic. They pursued Jews with less than total vigor. Occasionally, André Trocmé received midnight calls warning of raids in the morning. He would spread the word and avoid disaster. The commanding Vichy military officer, Major Julius Schmahling, pretended not to notice rescue efforts.

Nonetheless, André Trocmé and his assistant Édouard Theis were arrested in early 1943. They were released but hid in the hills. Magda kept up the couple's work alone until their return. The Jews remained uncaptured.

After the war, most Le Chambon residents refused praise. "How can you call us 'good'?" they would ask. "We were doing what had to be done."[2]

Rufino Niccacci

"I became a cheat and a liar," Father Rufino Niccacci recalled.[3] He was sure God forgave him. Niccacci's actions, after all, saved hundreds of lives.

Italy enjoyed a tradition of religious tolerance. Many Jews prospered there. They even achieved

Pastor André Trocmé (center) and associate Édouard Thies (right) on their release from an internment camp. Trocmé's church helped make the French village of Le Chambon-sur-Lignon a safe haven for hundreds of Jews. Pictured at the bottom are some of the many Jewish children who were saved from certain death by the residents of Le Chambon-sur-Lignon.

political success. In the 1920s, the president of the nation's highest court was Jewish.

At first Italy's fascist leader, Benito Mussolini, did not act against Jews. His ally, Adolf Hitler, made him pass anti-Jewish laws in 1938, but those laws were seldom enforced. Mussolini did not permit Italian Jews to be deported to death camps. Likewise, those in Italian-conquered territories were rescued. When Germans asked Italy to turn over Jewish refugees for "general mobilization of manpower,"[4] which meant slave labor camps, Mussolini refused.

A revolution overthrew Mussolini in 1943. A few months later, Nazis conquered the country. They restored Mussolini, but only as a puppet. German Nazis actually ran the government, which meant peril for Italian Jews.

Bishop Giuseppe Placido Nicolini acted quickly. He summoned Rufino Niccacci, who headed a monastery in Assisi. Niccacci agreed to hide refugees from Rome.

Suddenly, the population of local monasteries and convents grew. Unfamiliar "monks" suddenly appeared. The convent hosted its first male visitors in seven hundred years. These visitors were Jewish, and the mother superior forbade entry to Nazi soldiers.

Some Jews blended into the community. The local printer, Luigi Brizi, became an expert forger, working nonstop to produce false documents. Jews who could pass as Italian citizens could live more or less openly. Others had to hide in the hills.

Niccacci set up two schools. Youngsters attended one school so that they would not fall behind in their studies. The other helped adults act like Christians so that they would not attract attention. Although the schools taught the Jews Christian rituals, they did not attempt to convert them to Christianity.

Although Italy's fascist leader Benito Mussolini (left) was an ally of Adolf Hitler's, he did not allow the deportation of Italian Jews to death camps.

Niccacci made several courageous moves. Bishop Nicolini once asked him to transport fifteen Jews to a nearby town. Niccacci went to the local military commander, Lieutenant Colonel Müller. He told Müller he had fifteen religious pilgrims who needed to return home. Could he borrow the colonel's truck to transport them? The colonel lent him the vehicle.

By 1944, the Allies were gaining control of Italy. The Nazis clearly were defeated. Even so, local police captured a sixteen-year-old Jew, although they had not arrested the town's Jews before. An infuriated Niccacci

went to the police chief. He reminded the chief that Allied forces would soon reach Assisi, and would deal harshly with the chief if the youth was hurt. "I am speaking to you not only as a priest, threatening you with God's punishment for the boy's execution. You ought to consider your future, not only in heaven, but also on earth," Niccacci said.[5] The tactic worked. The police chief released the boy.

Like the Trocmés in France, Niccacci received unspoken help. The SS left town in June 1944. Assisi's six hundred Jewish refugees had remained untouched. Just before he left, Lieutenant Colonel Müller visited St. Francis Church. He asked Niccacci to forgive him for his suspicions about the priest's activities. Müller said, "That SS captain really made me believe that you were hiding people wanted by our authorities." Addressing the others in the room, he added, "Imagine, that silly young fool insisting that your poor Padre Rufino was the head of Assisi's vast underground organization."[6] The monks in the room, along with several Jews disguised as monks, laughed along with Müller.

The colonel was no fool. Years later a journalist interviewed Müller's son. Had the colonel been aware of what was happening? The son responded, "He suspected it, and if he was deceived by the Italian underground, it is because he wanted to be deceived."[7]

Father Marie-Benoît

Monsignor Jules-Gérard Saliège, archbishop of Toulouse, France, openly challenged the puppet French government the Germans had established. When the Vichy government began deporting Jews, a pastoral letter from Saliège opposed the move. It declared, "Jews are men. Jews are women. They form part of the family of mankind. They are our brothers, a fact that Christians must not forget."[8] The "Saliège bomb," as

the letter became known, put the archbishop's life in constant danger.

Vichy officials were enraged by the letter. But common French people heeded the message. A Marseilles monk, Father Marie-Benoît, helped four thousand Jewish refugees escape to Spain and Switzerland.

Benoît used hundreds of contacts. An average-looking farmhand or dockworker might be a key link to the French underground and freedom. Benoît himself created thousands of documents that changed Jewish names into typical French ones. His assistant, Fernande Leboucher, recalled, "Night and day, Father Benoît was churning out forged identity cards and baptismal certificates, made out in the names of various nonexistent Durands, Duponts, and Duvals. . . . A single false move . . . would have brought the whole affair to the attention of the authorities, and—if we were lucky—we would then have spent the rest of the war in prison camps."[9]

Fernande Leboucher's husband, a Jew, had been captured by the Nazis. She appealed to Benoît for help and became his collaborator. Leboucher helped in a variety of ways. Before the war, she had been a noted fashion designer. When the war began, she opened a boutique. It sold high-priced, perhaps overpriced, clothing. Profits from the store went to Benoît's rescues. She also walked the streets as a courier of information. Leboucher had a variety of scarves. Each color meant a different message from Benoît to resistance members in Marseilles.

By the end of 1942, Allied troops had a foothold in northern Africa. This made southern France vulnerable to attack. Adolf Hitler took no chances. He took direct control of France. Benoît likewise took no chances. He fled France and went to Rome.

The monk continued his work in the Italian capital. He got ration cards and false documents for thousands of Jews around the city. One observer claimed that at times Vatican City, headquarters of the Roman Catholic Church, had more refugee Jews than Christians.[10]

In July 1943, Benoît tried to persuade the Pope to transfer French Jews to safety in northern Africa. This plan failed, but other plans were major successes. Italy had taken over a region of southern France. Benoît feared that Germans would grab this French area and deport Jews. He helped Jews move to Italy and to relative safety.

5

Leave These People Alone

Adolf Hitler's German Nazis conquered much of Europe. They could have conquered even more. But some European nations, including Spain, Portugal, Sweden, and Switzerland, remained neutral. Hitler respected that neutrality.

Despite its atrocities elsewhere, the Nazi government wished to maintain relations with the neutral countries. It recognized visas and passes from other nations. Most governments would not issue documents to help Jews. But renegade diplomats from several nations defied their governments. As a result, they saved thousands of Jewish lives.

Aristides de Sousa Mendes

By mid-1940, thousands of French residents were in a state of panic. They had to escape, but to where? Neutral Portugal had offered asylum (safety) to refugees of whatever political or religious belief. That policy changed in May. The Portuguese government told consuls in France that visas could only be issued to people with a specific destination in Portugal. No visas at all could be issued to Jews.

Most Portuguese consuls obeyed the order. Aristides de Sousa Mendes, Portuguese consul in Bordeaux, did not. He claimed that his nation's constitution allowed asylum to anyone. The government gave him a direct order to stop his activities. Nonetheless, he and his nephew Cesar continued issuing visas, thousands of them. Soon the consulate became packed with visa-seekers. Cesar recalled, "The dining room, the drawing room, and the Consul's offices were at the disposal of the refugees, dozens of them of both sexes. . . . They slept on chairs, on the floor, on the rugs. Everything was out of control."[1]

When the government recalled Sousa Mendes, he continued to rescue Jews. On the way to Portugal, he stopped at Bayonne. He saw a large crowd of refugees outside the vice-consul's office. The vice-consul there refused to issue visas. Although he had been removed from his post, Sousa Mendes still technically outranked the vice-consul. He took over and issued several hundred more visas. Even at the Spanish border, he granted visas to refugees.

All together, it is estimated that Sousa Mendes might have granted visas to thirty thousand refugees. Israeli historian Yehuda Bauer claimed Sousa Mendes led "perhaps the largest rescue action by a single individual during the Holocaust."[2]

Sempo Sugihara

One day in July 1940, Sempo Sugihara received an unusual request. A Dutch yeshiva (Jewish school) student was seeking entry to the Caribbean island of Curaçao. What did this have to do with Sugihara, a Japanese consul in Kovno, Lithuania?

The student had learned that no visa was necessary to enter Curaçao. However, he could not travel through Nazi-dominated Europe. He could travel through the Soviet Union and then to Japan if he had a Japanese transit visa for Curaçao.

Tropical islands hardly mattered to the Dutch student. He just wanted a pass to get out of Kovno. The student rightly feared that his life would be in danger if he stayed there. Sugihara, ignoring rules from his government, issued the visa. He later explained, "I cannot allow these people to die, people who [come] to me for help with death staring them in the eyes."[3]

The student advised his friends. Soon Sugihara was working night and day to issue phony travel papers. The Japanese government recalled him in early August.

Disobeying the orders of the Japanese government, diplomat Sempo Sugihara issued some two thousand visas to Polish Jews. These visas allowed the Poles to escape likely death in Europe.

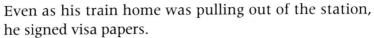

Even as his train home was pulling out of the station, he signed visa papers.

Sugihara's efforts saved as many as ten thousand Lithuanian Jews. Many settled in Shanghai, China, for the duration of the war. Among those Sugihara saved were a future Israeli religious affairs minister and a future speaker of the Knesset (Israeli congress).

Giorgio Perlasca

Giorgio Perlasca was an Italian fascist. He had fought with General Francisco Franco in the Spanish civil war. Hitler's Germany had backed Franco in that war. Ironically, Perlasca's service would help stop Hitler's murder plans.

Perlasca worked as a representative for an Italian company in Hungary. He kept contacts with the Spanish embassy in Budapest. When Mussolini fell in 1943, Perlasca was arrested. But Perlasca remembered that Franco had offered Spanish citizenship to those who fought for him in the war. He sought and received Spanish citizenship. This led to his release from prison.

In October 1944, Perlasca witnessed Nazis murdering a Jewish child on a Budapest street. The unbelievable sight changed his life. When the Spanish envoy left Budapest in late 1944, Perlasca posed as his replacement. He established safe houses for Jews under the Spanish flag, including one for children. He explained, "I simply cannot understand why a man can be persecuted simply because he is [of] a different religion than mine."[4]

Perlasca defied Hungarian authorities. When Hungarian Nazis came to a safe house to take the Jews, Perlasca said, "You must leave these people alone. I am . . . the flag."[5] The interior minister declared that all Jews in foreign missions would be taken out and killed. Perlasca answered that if that happened, three thousand

Hungarians in Spain would be arrested. He had no authority from the Spanish government to make such a statement, but the bluff worked. The interior minister withdrew his threat.

U.S. Involvement

For most of Hitler's rule, the United States did little to rescue European Jews. Americans had organized the Évian Conference, but with the purpose of persuading other nations to accept refugees. President Franklin D. Roosevelt looked the other way when the S.S. *St. Louis* sought a port. American planes could have bombed railroad tracks leading to Auschwitz. Assistant Secretary of War John J. McCloy rejected three proposals to bomb Auschwitz. McCloy wrote, "Such an effort, even if practicable, might provoke even more vindictive action by the Germans."[6] Neither he nor anyone else explained what could be more harmful than the daily murder of thousands of innocent civilians.

American government officials had long been aware of the Holocaust. Reliable sources in Switzerland relayed reports of Jewish extermination to the State Department. Instead of working for rescue, the State Department suppressed the report. It sent out cables forbidding consulates in neutral countries from accepting reports of atrocities against Jews.

Treasury Department lawyers found these State Department messages in late 1943. They threatened to make them public. If it were shown that President Roosevelt knew of mass murder and did nothing, the political results would be disastrous. Only then did the administration take rescue action.

The direct action was very little. The United States chose one thousand refugees, mostly Jews, from southern Italy. Each had to sign a document promising to return to their homeland after the war. Survivor Adam

Minz said, "We would have signed almost anything [to escape Europe]."[7] All were sent to a former military camp in Oswego, New York, in August 1944. They spent the rest of the war there.

Pressure on the State Department produced one positive result. The government created the War Refugee Board in early 1944. It was charged with planning a rescue policy for Europe's refugees. Funds had to come from private sources. Jewish and other humanitarian groups obliged. Then all they needed was someone to carry out the board's rescues. They found the right person in Raoul Wallenberg.

Raoul Wallenberg

Years after the war, a survivor remembered his most frightening moment. When he was a child, Nazis had come to his house to remove his mother. The boy had been left alone for two or three hours. Miraculously, his mother had returned. He had asked how she survived.

"She said one word: 'Wallenberg.' I knew immediately what she meant," the survivor recalled.[8]

The most legendary hero of the Jewish rescuers was an unlikely one. Athletic, handsome, and wealthy, the Swede Raoul Wallenberg could have remained in his homeland during the war. Instead, he risked his life daily in Hungary.

Even though Hungary was a German ally, the government would not participate in the Final Solution. As

Swedish diplomat Raoul Wallenberg (top) saved the lives of tens of thousands of Hungarian Jews in 1944. The Soviets detained him in early 1945, and he was never seen in the West again. In the bottom picture, Raoul Wallenberg, standing on the right with his hands clasped, tries to aid a group of Jews assembled at a train station in Budapest.

a result, Hungary had the only large Jewish population left in Europe. About eight hundred thousand Jews had survived in the central European nation.

By 1944, the outcome of the war was obvious. Sooner or later, Germany would lose. For some Nazi leaders, that outcome was no longer important. They wanted to kill as many Jews as possible before the war ended.

One such fanatic was Adolf Eichmann. The high-ranking SS official was assigned to Hungary. He tried to order the deportation of the nation's Jews. Hungary's leader, Miklós Horthy de Nagybánya, refused to allow it. The Nazis would not take such disobedience from a so-called ally. They forced Horthy to install a puppet government. Eichmann then started a Jewish evacuation. He ordered more than four hundred thousand Hungarian Jews moved to Auschwitz from May until July. No other country had so many Jews killed so fast.

Raoul Wallenberg had worked in Hungary and had business connections there. He spoke fluent Hungarian and German. Wallenberg had met with the War Refugee Board and agreed to help save Jews. He had demanded certain conditions. He would be free to come and go as he pleased. He would have to answer to no one. He would have all the money he needed.

When the board agreed to those conditions, he set to work. He traveled lightly, with only a hat and knapsack. In his pocket he kept a revolver. He carried the gun "not because I intended ever to use it, but to give myself courage."[9] Wallenberg begged when he needed to beg, bribed when he needed to bribe, threatened when he needed to threaten, and blackmailed when he needed to blackmail. As a result, he extended diplomatic protection to two hundred thousand Hungarian Jews.

Wallenberg set up an office. Then he began issuing fake passports. These were no ordinary pieces of paper.

Wallenberg figured that the fancier the document was, the more likely it would be to fool German soldiers. His yellow-and-blue Swedish passports contained a three-crown seal of the king. Seals, stamps, and signatures filled the document. The text read,

> The Royal Swedish Legation in Budapest certifies that the above-signed will be traveling to Sweden with the Royal Swedish Foreign Ministry's authorization. His name has also been registered on the Collective Passport. Until departure, he and his living quarters fall under the protection of the Royal Swedish Legation in Budapest.[10]

Then he obtained housing for the legation. Jewish families donated some houses for the duration of the war. Wallenberg purchased others. Jews by the thousands moved into these havens. Living conditions were hardly perfect, but they beat the risk of deportation from living on the streets. Wallenberg also set up soup kitchens and a hospital for the legation houses. He recruited a staff of four hundred people to help him.

Other nations followed Wallenberg's example. Several Latin American countries issued visa papers. Spain gave papers to descendants of Spanish Jews ousted from Spain centuries before. Papal representative Angelo Roncalli issued thousands of baptismal certificates and safe-conduct passes.

Wallenberg saved Jews whenever, wherever, and however he could. On one occasion, as he passed a train station, he saw Jews being loaded on a train for death camps. He demanded that all Jews with passports leave the train. The prisoners waved anything—driver's licenses, eyeglass prescriptions, even deportation papers—at him. He honored all documents as passports and saved three hundred lives.

Sometimes Wallenberg used influence with the high and mighty. When he heard that the new government of Hungary would no longer honor protection of Jews from neutral nations, he acted quickly. He went to Baroness Elisabeth Kemény, wife of the minister of foreign affairs. He had met her at diplomatic functions. He also knew that her parents were Jewish. Wallenberg reminded the baroness that the Soviet army was approaching Budapest. They would look kindly on those who opposed Nazis and unfavorably on those who helped them. He also told her he knew of her Jewish origins. The baroness went to her husband, and the baron went to Hungary's new political leader. The protection orders remained.

Wallenberg had a protector of sorts. Germany valued its relationship with the neutral Swedish government. Sweden acted as a go-between with the Nazis and the Allied nations of Great Britain and France. If Germany lost the war, Sweden would have to act on the Germans' behalf. It would not do so if a Swedish diplomat were hurt. Eichmann's superior, Heinrich Himmler, was trying to negotiate a secret peace with the Allies. Thus Eichmann knew that a bullet through Wallenberg's heart might mean a noose around his own neck.

That protection did not extend to Jews. In late 1944, Eichmann ordered a roundup of all Jewish men age sixteen to sixty. Fifty thousand of the able-bodied were led on a three-day march to a forced-labor location outside Budapest, to dig trenches for the Nazis. The women and children were forced on a march to the

Adolf Eichmann oversaw the deportation of 3 million Jews to extermination camps.

Austrian border, 120 miles away, in freezing cold and with little food. Those who did not die from the march would perish in a death camp. Wallenberg could not save all of those Jews, but he and his aides followed the "death marchers," offering food, medicine, and clothing where they could.

Wallenberg was able to issue a few passports to the marchers. Miriam Herzog, then seventeen years old, remembered the day. "Suddenly I heard a great commotion among the women. 'It's Wallenberg,' they said. . . . He said to them: 'Please, you must forgive me, but I cannot help all of you. I can only provide certificates for a hundred of you.'"[11]

Herzog was one of the lucky hundred. They were hidden in a cattle truck on a train and transported back to Budapest. "I don't know how Wallenberg managed it; I suppose he must have bribed the railway officials and guards," she said. "But we were alive—and it was thanks entirely to Wallenberg."[12]

6

Danes Helping Fellow Danes

The fate of the Jews usually depended upon their neighbors. These neighbors varied from nation to nation. Every country had heroes who tried to save Jews and Nazi collaborators who would betray them. In some lands local populations worked with the Nazis to destroy the Jews. But in one country, nearly everyone—from the king to the poorest fisherman—helped in a nationwide rescue.

"Throwing Away Sour Beer"

Why did some countries try harder to save Jews than other ones?

There were several factors. Many Jews in Eastern Europe spoke a different language (Yiddish) than their neighbors. They wore different clothing. Where Jews were visibly different from Christians, the Christians were less likely to aid them.

Christian churches in some countries encouraged discrimination. They preserved the image of Jews as killers of Christ. Other churches stressed similarities between Christianity and Judaism. These churches believed mass murder of any kind was wrong.

The Slovakian church actively supported mass murder. That attitude flowed to the local population. Adolf Eichmann claimed that Slovakia gave away its Jews like someone "throwing away sour beer."[1]

Similar results occurred in other countries where the church made no resistance. Four out of five Lithuanian Jews died; there was no protest. By the end of 1942, nine-tenths of Poland's Jews had been killed.

Even where there was no church opposition, danger to Jews existed. Switzerland declared itself a neutral nation, but that neutrality seemed to take pro-Nazi tones. The Swiss government excluded Jews from 1938 until 1944. It even insisted that passports of German Jews be distinctively marked. Thus their passports had a large *J* stamped on them. Any refugee without papers was sent home immediately—even if home meant a trip to a death camp.

The Swiss government declared, "Refugees for racial reasons alone are not political refugees."[2] After France fell to the Nazis, Switzerland stated, "French Jews are to be turned back without exception because they are in no danger in their own country."[3] The French Jews believed differently. Many risked their lives and spent their fortunes to get near the border. From there, they hired smugglers to bring them into Switzerland. About twenty-eight thousand Jews fled to the mountain nation.

Italians, Dutch, and Bulgarians

In 1943, when Germany set up a puppet government in Italy after Benito Mussolini's fall, the Jews of Italy were in danger. Within fourteen months of the creation of the puppet government, eight thousand Jews were shipped to concentration camps. Most of them perished. However, thanks to rescuers such as Rufino Niccacci, who found hiding places for others, 80 percent of Italian Jews survived the war.

Dutch Jews did not fare as well. Well-meaning efforts on their behalf might have hurt them. The Netherlands enjoyed a long history of religious freedom. Most Dutch Protestants and Catholics supported their Jewish neighbors. When Nazis shipped 425 Jews to a concentration camp, workers organized a nationwide strike. It was the only strike in occupied Europe on behalf of Jews.

The strike lasted only two days. Nazis threatened even greater actions against Jews if the strike continued. The Amsterdam *Judenrat* (Jewish council) urged everyone to return to work. Nazis used the strike as an excuse to round up resistance leaders, which set back the resistance cause. Neighboring Belgium, where the Comite de Defense des Juifs operated, saved many of Holland's Jewish residents, but three quarters of Dutch Jews died at Nazi hands.

Less than one percent of Bulgaria's population was Jewish. For years, they experienced no discrimination. Jews, Muslims, Catholics, and Orthodox Christians lived together in the southeast European country.

Bulgaria allied itself with the Nazis early in the war. This pact allowed the Balkan nation to overrun neighboring Thrace and Macedonia. Several hundred Jews lived in these captured territories.

King Boris of Bulgaria opposed Jewish deportation. However, he had to satisfy his Nazi allies. Bulgaria passed the Defense of the Nations in 1941. It forced Jews into detention camps outside the capital city of Sofia. The Bulgarian Orthodox Church opposed the anti-Semitic measure. So did leading doctors, writers, and other professionals. Even though the law was enacted, it was not always enforced.

This law was not enough for Hitler and the German Nazis. They demanded Jewish prisoners for slave labor and death. Boris visited Hitler in Berlin in 1943. Under pressure, he turned over the Jews of Thrace and Macedonia. But the Bulgarian king refused to turn over his own nation's Jewish citizens. He told Hitler they were needed for road construction. Boris was stalling for time. He knew the Germans were losing the war.

Boris died a mysterious death shortly after the Berlin visit. By then, the German army was too weak to take action. Thanks to King Boris's determination, more than forty-eight thousand Bulgarian Jews survived the war.

"We Must All Be in Hiding"

Germans invaded Denmark with lightning speed on April 9, 1940. By the end of the day, the Scandinavian country had surrendered. The Danish government agreed to cooperate with the Nazi invaders. It had no choice.

Denmark got some peace terms. Danes would supply food for German troops and not oppose German occupiers. In turn, the Germans would respect Danish neutrality toward the Nazis. Danes would not be drafted to fight for the Nazis. Most important, Germany would not discriminate against Danish Jews.

Helen Yom Tov Herman and her mother, Ida, (top) survived the war by hiding on a German farm after fleeing from Poland. Members of the Boogaard family with two of the many Jewish children that they hid at one of their farms near Amsterdam (bottom). In addition to hiding Jews, the Boogaard family also hid members of the Dutch resistance by sheltering them in a series of underground dwellings.

The Jewish population in Denmark was a tiny one. Less than one percent of all Danes practiced the faith. Jews and Christians had lived there peacefully for centuries. Christians called Jews friends, classmates, business partners, even husbands or wives. They did not see them as Jews living in Denmark. Instead, they were Danes who happened to be Jewish.

At first, Hitler tolerated the Danish Jews' freedom. He admired the Danes and considered most to be fellow Aryans. He needed the products from their farms and factories. Besides, the Danes posed no threat. There were more powerful enemies now. If Hitler wanted to kill Danish Jews, he could do so later.

In some respects, the occupation was a good-natured one. German soldiers liked the assignment in Denmark. They met friendly people and ate good food. It was certainly better than freezing on the Russian front. Even Denmark's King Christian X responded in gentle humor. Hitler suggested that they combine the governments of their two countries. The beloved king replied, "I have given your suggestion much thought. But at my age, I think I am too old to rule over two countries."[4]

The king never wavered in his defense of the Jews. When a Nazi officer talked of the "Jewish question," he responded, "There is no Jewish question in this country. There is only my people."[5] Nazis threatened to make Danish Jews wear the Star of David on their clothing. According to legend, King Christian pledged that he would don a star as well.

Denmark's underground spread news but did little more. Some members favored active opposition to the Nazis. Others favored a wait-and-see attitude. They believed active resistance would bring Nazi retaliation. Jews would be the first victims.

Events in 1943 helped change their attitudes. Allied victories in the Soviet Union, Africa, and the Pacific highlighted German weaknesses. Danes overwhelmingly rejected their nation's Nazi party in the spring elections. German Nazis demanded a change in Danish production, from food to war materials. August strikes in Copenhagen and Odense infuriated the Nazis.

The Nazis retaliated. They declared martial law and took away Danes' rights. King Christian was placed under palace arrest. The Danish government resigned in protest.

Dr. Werner Best was the Nazi political leader in Denmark. At first, he did not move against Jews. By August 1943, Hitler demanded action. On September 8, Best suggested the arrest and deportation of Jews. Hitler agreed. A few days later, Nazis stole a list of Jews in Denmark.

However, Best made another move. He detailed plans to German shipping executive Georg Ferdinand Duckwitz. German ships would dock at Copenhagen on September 29, he told Duckwitz. Raids would take place October 1 and 2.

Perhaps Best hoped Duckwitz would alert Danish authorities. If so, he got his wish. Duckwitz wrote in his diary on September 19, "I know what I have to do."[6] Then he did it.

Duckwitz told Hans Hedtoft, head of Denmark's Social Democratic party, about the raid. Hedtoft went to C. B. Henriques, leader of the country's Jewish community. Henriques replied, "You lie. It can't be true. I don't believe it."[7] Marcus Melchior, Denmark's leading rabbi, believed it. Jews flocked to the Copenhagen synagogue September 30 for a Jewish New Year's service. Melchior gave them an unexpected message: "Tomorrow the Germans plan to raid Jewish homes throughout Copenhagen to arrest all the Danish Jews for shipment to concentration camps," he warned. "The situation is very serious. We must take action immediately. You must leave the synagogue now and contact all relatives, friends and neighbors. . . . By nightfall tonight we must all be in hiding."[8]

Jews and Gentiles alike spread the message. Students told professors. Patients told doctors. Customers told shopkeepers. Neighbors told neighbors. People told friends and total strangers. An ambulance driver named Jorgen Knudsen grabbed a directory from a telephone booth. He circled every name that appeared Jewish, then went to warn each family. When some of the Jews became afraid, he took them to a local doctor.

On October 1, the raids began. Most Danish policemen did not participate. They supported their countrymen, not Hitler. The *Wehrmacht* (regular German army) troops often allowed Jews to escape. They would knock on a Jew's door but walk away if no one answered. Best himself issued orders forbidding Germans from breaking into Jewish homes. Those who pursued Jews with less than full vigor usually came back empty-handed.

The Jews escaped. Within hours, they had transferred property titles to friends. They fled to Christian friends' homes, summer homes, barns, warehouses, convents, and churches. Some remained in Copenhagen. Doctors there "discharged" Jewish patients and "admitted" patients with Christian names. Several hundred Jews fled to fields outside Copenhagen. Student groups pursued them and led them to safer hiding places. In all, thousands of people helped the Jews escape. They provided food, shelter, transportation, information, and money. Danes left messages for would-be informers that their lives would be in danger if they helped turn in Danish Jews.

Christians spoke out in defense of Jews. Danish bishops issued a statement that was read from pulpits on October 3. "Wherever Jews are persecuted because of their religion or race it is the duty of the Christian Church to protest . . . ," the statement read. "We must obey God before we obey man."[9]

Some frightened Jews committed suicide. Most waited patiently. But they could not remain in hiding forever. Somehow, they had to reach safety. Then they received a break.

"Valkommen!"

Sweden had declared itself a neutral nation. At some places, the Swedish coast was less than three miles from Danish islands. But the German-controlled coast guard made escape there almost impossible. Sweden was so near yet seemed so far away.

Worst of all, Sweden had questionable neutrality. The government allowed German troops to pass through the nation. It sold iron ore to Germany. The Swedish government would not accept fugitive Danes. But by 1943, Sweden saw how the war was turning.

Niels Bohr escaped to Sweden on September 30. The United States sought the services of Denmark's most famous physicist. His work would be invaluable in developing an atomic bomb.

Bohr, a Nobel prizewinner, would not leave Sweden until it offered a haven to Danish Jews. The Swedish king gave his word that the Jews would be welcomed. That was not enough. The king's announcement had to be printed on the front pages of Sweden's leading newspapers and broadcast over the radio. Sweden, perhaps because of American pressure, followed Bohr's wishes.

Danish Jews headed for the coast. Members of the underground helped them reach seaside towns. Often, the refugee Jews did not know these helpers by name. They only knew "the farmer," "the young man," "a lady," or "a friendly family."[10]

One bookstore in Copenhagen served as a head-quarters. If a certain poetry book was displayed in the window, it was safe for Jews to enter. Once inside the store, a courier would lead them to coastal safety. The store became so busy with refugees that the owners became irritated whenever anyone came in to buy a book.

Lucky refugees at the town of Elsinore got a boxcar ride. Sweden ferried boxcars full of iron ore to Denmark and Germany. When the cars returned to Sweden, they were empty. Danes at first sneaked Jews onto the cars, and they rode to Swedish safety. These shipments worked until a Swedish newspaper described the plan. It had to be abandoned.

The Helsinger Sewing Club kept busy at this time. It had nothing to do with tailors or seamstresses. This and other "clubs" were code names for evacuation missions involving hundreds of fishermen.

Fishing boats carried the most Jews to Sweden. The fishermen usually charged money for these trips. A few demanded outrageous sums, but some charged nothing. Most received $20 to $60 per head. No one was left behind because they could not pay. Danes raised about $600,000 to finance the informal rescue fleet.

Boats left at night from deserted coves. Many carried ten to twenty people. Passengers waited for hours. Then they would see a light in the distance. This brief signal meant action. They waded a hundred yards through icy waters to the boat. Occasionally a German patrol would encounter people waiting for a ride. Underground members, fishermen, and even Danish police usually chased them away.

Fishermen and refugees alike risked their lives. Patrol boats and harbor mines posed dire threats. If the human-made hazards did not stop the rescue boats, the storms might. However, the fishermen got some unofficial support. One German coast guard commander ordered all his boats to dock. While they received little-needed repairs, Danes ferried refugees to safety.

Nazis sometimes boarded the boats. A few carried dogs trained to sniff out people. One Dane solved this problem by creating a powder made from dried blood and cocaine. The mixture deadened the dogs' sense of smell.

When science failed, plain nerve took over. Peter Christopher Hansen made a run with ten Jews inside his boat's hold. Ten Nazis boarded his vessel. Hansen ordered them off. If they did not leave immediately, he said, he would report them to their superiors. They left.

Danger came in many forms. Midway through their ride, the fisherman carrying Rabbi Melchior's family lost his nerve. He started to head back to Denmark. The rabbi knocked down the fisherman, took control of the boat, and steered it to Sweden.

For passengers, the ride was nerve-racking. "I counted the minutes," recalled evacuee Herbert Pundik. "From the time we left Denmark . . . to the moment the fisherman called us on deck and told us that we were safe, exactly thirty-seven minutes had passed."[11]

One boat had to stop its engine to elude a German patrol boat. A gale blew it off course. At daylight, the passengers saw land. But which land was it? A passenger recalled,

> The boat approached the coast; we hoped that liberty was at hand. We were really in Swedish territorial waters. The Danish flag was raised and people threw their arms around one another and cried for joy. . . . The harbor we had sailed into was full of Swedish warships

on whose decks sailors waved and shouted *'Valkommen'* ['Welcome'].[12]

The fishermen succeeded. Of about 7,800 Jews in Denmark, more than 7,200 made it to Sweden. Most of the rest were either old or ill. Even most of those captured by Nazis fared well. They were shipped to the "model" camp at Theresienstadt (called Terezin in Czech), where conditions were better than at most other camps. The Danish government constantly asked about their condition. Friends from Denmark sent them food packages. None were sent to death camps. In all, less than 2 percent of Danish Jews died because of the Nazis.

Non-Jewish Danes helped the Jews. In turn, the Jews helped the Danish spirit. Underground member Jørgen Kieler said, "I am not sure that the Danish Resistance Movement would have gained the strength which it actually did had it not been for the inspiration we received from the Jews."[13]

Several factors led to the rescue's success. Danish Jews were close to a neutral haven. A top German official (Duckwitz) spilled the deportation secret. German troops helped refugees, or at least ignored escape attempts. But these factors would have meant little without the efforts of the Danish people. They followed their consciences and aided their neighbors. Evacuee Leif Donde commented, "It was a question of Danes helping fellow Danes in a time of need."[14]

Danish fishermen ferry a load of Jewish refugees to safety in neutral Sweden (top). An informal rescue fleet helped save some seven thousand Danish Jews. A Danish escapee leaves his hiding place once the fishing boat reaches Swedish waters (bottom). Danish fishermen helped save nearly all of Denmark's Jewish population.

7

Bear Witness to This Terrible Nightmare

Heroism took many forms during the Holocaust. For many people, it took great courage even to describe the horrors they faced. Keeping diaries and producing underground newspapers were punishable by death.

Yet some people insisted on keeping records. A common prayer in the camps proclaimed, "God, let there be survivors who can bear witness to this terrible nightmare."[1] When prisoners themselves did not survive, their documents sometimes did.

Many wanted to make sure that others would know of Nazi atrocities. Other people kept diaries only for personal reasons. They probably did not believe that anyone else would read them. Yet one of those diaries, written by young Anne Frank, became the most famous document of the Holocaust.

"We Don't Forget Anything"

Countless Jews survived the Holocaust from sheer willpower. An inner strength helped them live so that they could tell their stories. Auschwitz escapee Alfred Wetzler wrote, "We don't forget anything, we shall do our best to tell the world what monstrous crimes against humanity the Nazis are committing."[2] Wetzler and fellow escapee Walter Rosenberg (later known as Rudolf Vrba) produced a report on those atrocities. They distributed two thousand copies, including some sent to Great Britain and the United States.

Hirsh Kadushin preserved the horrors in a different way. He bought a small camera and secretly photographed all aspects of ghetto life in the Lithuanian town of Kovno. "I don't have a gun. . . . My camera will be my revenge," he claimed.[3]

"Our existence as a people will not be destroyed. Individuals will be destroyed, but the Jewish community will live on."[4] Teacher Chaim Kaplan wrote that comment in his diary in 1939. He is believed to have been killed in the Treblinka death camp, but his words survived.

Kaplan lived in Warsaw, Poland. At one time Warsaw boasted the largest and liveliest Jewish community in the world. Slowly but surely it was being destroyed. Kaplan saw Jews being stripped of their rights and property. They were forced to ride separate streetcars. They had to wear the Jewish star on their clothing. Then they were made to live in a ghetto, an isolated part of the city. Kaplan commented, "Will it be a closed ghetto? . . . A closed ghetto means gradual death. An open ghetto is only a halfway catastrophe."[5]

Teenager Mary Berg was another Warsaw ghetto resident. In one respect, she was more fortunate than most. Her mother was a non-Jewish American citizen. They kept an American Citizen sign on their door. That saved them from the involuntary labor forced upon their neighbors.

Mary's diary captured the misery of the ghetto. She was afraid to go to school because she might get hit by a bullet. Children, she wrote, "are more like monkeys than children. They no longer beg for bread, but for death."[6] Mary also shared the few isolated joys. "Today is my birthday," she wrote on October 10, 1942. "Tonight my sister managed to snatch three turnips, and we had a real feast to celebrate the occasion."[7]

Mary Berg was one of the lucky ones. Nazis released her and her mother in early 1943. Few ghetto residents were so fortunate. One who perished was a different kind of hero, Dr. Janusz Korczak.

Korczak was already a hero among Jews and Poles. The famed educator had written many books starring heroic King Matt. He ran the Jewish orphanage in the Warsaw ghetto. Korczak refused many opportunities to escape the ghetto. He remained with, and cared for, his children.

In August 1942, the children were called for deportation. Korczak dressed them in their best clothes, lined them up in rows of four, then marched them silently to the plaza. One child carried the flag of King Matt. The orphans were soon executed, and so was he. Their quiet, dignified protest, however, inspired other Warsaw residents.

Berg's diary helped preserve his memory. "He was the pride of the ghetto," she wrote. "His children's home gave us courage. . . . He devoted all his life, all his creative work as educator and writer, to the poor children of Warsaw. Even at the last moment, he refused to be separated from them."[8]

Vedem

In any age, Petr Ginz would be called a genius. At the age of thirteen, he wrote a novel. At fourteen, he made abstract paintings. He wrote essays on philosophy and

Janusz Korczak talks with a group of students at his Warsaw orphanage. Instead of taking opportunities to flee Warsaw's ghetto, he accompanied his orphans to their death.

edited a magazine at fifteen. But by the time he was sixteen, he was dead.

Ginz was part of an upper-middle-class family in Prague, Czechoslovakia. Nazis moved him and fifteen thousand other Jewish children to a concentration camp in Terezin. The former army camp was designed to hold four thousand people. Under the Nazis, it held fifty thousand. More than thirty-three thousand would die there. Another eighty-seven thousand were sent from there to death camps in the East.

Young people at the camp did not idly await doom. Petr's sister, Chava Ginz Pressburger, recalled, "They wrote, they drew, and they hoped, and their solace was in their creative activity."[9]

A magazine called *Vedem* (meaning "in the lead" in Czech) was the result of their activity. It was the most exclusive magazine in the world. Only one copy was made each week. That copy never got beyond the camp. *Vedem* contained a variety of articles, pictures, poems, and essays. Sidney Taussig sneaked into the camp's cremation chamber and then described it in the magazine. George Brady wrote, "Every day I have hunger for lunch, followed later by fear of the east of Poland."[10] Ginz pined for his hometown of Prague. "I have long since forgotten those shady nooks and sleepy canals. How are they? They cannot be grieving for me as I do for them."[11]

In late 1944, Nazis shipped Petr Ginz to Auschwitz. He arrived on Yom Kippur, the holiest day of the Jewish year, and died soon afterward. Shortly after Ginz's deportation, Taussig buried all copies of *Vedem*. He returned and dug them up years later.

Journalist Ed Serotta commented about Ginz and his young colleagues: "[They] fought back against all odds and they fought with the tools their parents have given them: courage, ethics, optimism."[12]

Tales from the Milk Cans

Most diaries and records of the Holocaust were individual efforts. One historian, however, led a group project. Thanks to Emmanuel Ringelblum, dozens of Warsaw ghetto residents preserved their thoughts. It was an invaluable record of the struggles they faced.

The historian began collecting information in May 1940. Any document might be worth saving. He took underground newspapers, reports from resistance groups, testimonies by death camp survivors, and notices from the *Judenrat* (Jewish council). He preserved posters, residents' diaries, and specially requested papers discussing aspects of ghetto life. Artists, teachers, rabbis, and writers contributed. The secret operation became known as *Oneg Shabbat* ("Joy of the Sabbath").

Those documents included Ringelblum's own observations. In November 1940, Germans built a wall around the ghetto. Soon afterward he recorded, "A Christian was killed . . . for throwing a sack of bread over the wall."[13] After a massive deportation of Jews, he lamented, "Why didn't we resist when they began to resettle 300,000 Jews from Warsaw? Why did we allow ourselves to be led like sheep to the slaughter?"[14]

Ringelblum knew his chances of survival were practically zero. However, he wanted to make sure the documents were saved. He and friends hid them in three milk cans, then buried them under Warsaw streets. Two of the milk cans were recovered after the war. Although Ringelblum was executed by Nazis in 1944, his legacy survives.

Anne Frank

No one would be interested in "the musings of a thirteen-year-old schoolgirl," Anne Frank wrote.[15] She was wrong. Fifty years later, her diary had been translated into dozens of languages and read by millions of people. Her life story became the subject of movies and a Broadway play. Anne Frank's diary became perhaps the most famous document of the Holocaust and made Anne its most beloved young victim.

Frank, with her sister and parents, and four others, hid from the Nazis. For two years, they stayed in the attic of an Amsterdam office building at 263 Prinsengracht.

Neighbors remembered Anne as a friendly, outgoing girl. Those qualities showed in the diary she kept. Anne began the thought book a month before her family went into hiding. She continued it until her capture. She wrote it as though writing a letter to a friend. "Dear Kitty" began each day's entry.

Nothing was more important to Anne than her diary. Her father realized what it meant to her. He ordered everyone to leave her alone when she wrote in it. No one was permitted to read it.

Anne felt completely free with her thoughts. She described the frightening move to her hiding place. She and her family had to walk across town in the pouring rain to safety without being noticed. "We put on heaps of clothes as if we were going to the North Pole, the sole reason being to take clothes with us," she wrote in July 1942. "No Jew in our situation would have dreamed of going out with a suitcase full of clothing."[16] From her window, she watched a November 1942 roundup. "I often see rows of good, innocent people accompanied by crying children, . . . bullied and knocked about until they almost drop. No one is spared . . . each and all join in the march of death."[17]

For its observations on the Holocaust alone, the diary would have been a valuable book. But Anne Frank's diary was much more. A typical girl, although more insightful than most, she opened her feelings to the world. Many of her feelings were common to any teenager. Adults sometimes bothered her, and she sometimes bothered them. She shared her first kiss with Peter, the shy boy from the other family in the attic.

Historian Emmanuel Ringelblum led a group project that preserved a written history of the Warsaw ghetto.

She was afraid her sister might steal his affections. "Relations between [all of] us are getting worse all the time," she wrote in September 1943. "At mealtimes, no one dares to open their mouths (except to allow a mouthful of food to slip in) because whatever is said you either annoy someone or it is misunderstood. . . . [W]e've almost forgotten how to laugh."[18]

Anne Frank allowed herself to be miserable in her diary words. She wrote in December 1943, "I couldn't help feeling a great longing to have lots of fun myself for once, and to laugh until my tummy ached."[19]

However, most of the time she remained optimistic. "In spite of everything, I still believe that people are really good at heart. . . . If I look up into the heavens, I think that it will all come right, that this cruelty too will end, and that peace and tranquility will return again," she wrote in July 1944.[20]

Those hopes did not come through for her. Less than a month after that entry, Anne and the others were captured by the Nazis. Anne died in the Bergen-Belsen concentration camp a few weeks before its 1945 liberation. Of those with whom she had been hiding, only her father, Otto Frank, survived the war.

Otto's associate, Miep Gies, had gathered Anne's diary and loose papers after the Nazis left. After the war, she gave them to Otto, and he passed copies to family members. Within two years, a publisher sold the book. In the half century since her death, millions have read her story. Anne Frank remains the symbol of talent and potential destroyed by the Holocaust.

Stood Up and Fought Like Lions

or many people, their image of Jews during the Holocaust is clear: They allowed themselves to be murdered without a struggle. In fact, thousands of Jews fought against the Nazis. They joined partisan (guerrilla) units, mainly in Eastern Europe.

"Some of Us Were Fighting"

Nazis outnumbered resistance fighters. They had more troops, and they had far more weapons. The only way partisans could fight was by hit-and-run warfare. They would strike a target, then hurry on to the next one. Partisans needed space where they would not be detected. Holland, with its flat farmland, could not hide partisan fighters. Heavily forested countries like Belorussia could provide shelter for them.

Single men of different religions comprised most partisan groups, although some single women also joined. Many partisans rejected children. It would have been too dangerous to care for them while fighting.

However, some family camps contained as many as ten thousand people. The partisans felt that helping camp members survive was at least as important as fighting Nazi soldiers. These family camps also helped the partisans. They provided tailors, blacksmiths, and other support services to the fighting troops.

Life was never easy for a partisan. Camps frequently moved from place to place. Most could not grow any food. They had to buy, beg, borrow, or steal it from neighboring peasants. They froze in winter and sweltered in summer. They always had to be alert for raids from Nazis.

For Jewish partisans, life was doubly difficult. They not only had to beware of Nazi enemies, but also had to watch their would-be allies. Jews in underground groups in Greece, Italy, Yugoslavia, and Bulgaria fought alongside non-Jewish partisans without trouble. Those in Poland, the Ukraine, Latvia, Lithuania, and Estonia often faced unfriendliness and even betrayal from local residents and other partisans. Many units would not accept Jews. Others took them in at first. Then they murdered them, raped them, or took their weapons.

"I stole two rifles and joined the partisans," Max Grosblat of the Polish Ukraine commented. "Not all the Jewish people went to death like sheep. Some of us were fighting."[1] Grosblat had escaped his ghetto and joined a group of Ukrainian partisans in 1943. They blew up bridges to stop trains carrying Nazi supplies and troops. The partisan group had a small airstrip in a forest clearing and radio contact with Moscow. At night, they built bonfires at the four corners of the airfield to enable weapons and supplies to be flown from Russia.

"There were very few Jews in the [partisan group], and [these partisans] killed a lot of Jews themselves," Grosblat commented. He recalled one Jewish refugee who did not want to admit he was Jewish. "[Some partisans] played a Jewish tune on the record player, and he was humming the tune, so they shot him."[2]

Faye Porter of Poland remembered one anti-Semitic commander. "His adjutant [assistant] came secretly and told us we should keep our guard double and not sleep because he wants to destroy us," she said. "The partisans killed [the commander] instead."[3]

Jews often set up separate partisan units. Misha Gildenman (known as "Uncle Misha") in Poland and Dr. Yehezkel Atlas and Tuvia Bielski of Belorussia led three of the most famed partisan groups. They served with particular bravery and ferocity. As Atlas told his troops, "Every additional day is not yours, but belongs to your murdered families. You must avenge them."[4] Former partisan Faye Schulman recalled, "Torn from the lives they had once known, [Jews] stood up and fought like lions."[5]

The Bielski Partisans

"I don't promise you anything. We may be killed while we try to live," said Tuvia Bielski when he formed his partisan group. "But we will do all we can to save more lives. This is our way, we don't select, we don't eliminate the old, the children, the women. Life is difficult, we are in danger all the time, but if we perish, . . . we die like human beings."[6]

Bielski and his family lived in the western Belorussian village of Stankewicze. At one time that area was claimed by the Soviets. Germans took it over early in the war. Bielski's parents and two of his brothers died at Nazi hands.

Nazis tried to force all the Jews of Belorussia to live in ghettos. Tuvia and his brother Zus refused. Instead they went to the large Naliboki forest. There they formed an *otriad* (partisan unit) in late 1942. Another brother, Asael, joined them a few months later. Tuvia commanded the *otriad*. Asael was in charge of day-to-day activities. Zus served as chief scout.

"We knew how to fight," Zus claimed. "We would not let others push us around. We were never afraid, that was the kind of family we were."[7] However, fighting was never the main purpose of the Bielski *otriad*. "The Germans caught my father, mother, and two brothers. They took them to the ghetto and from there they were taken to their death," Tuvia explained. He added, "So would I imitate them, just by killing some Germans, any Germans? . . . To me it made no sense. I wanted to save [lives], not to kill. . . . [Jews] did listen to me, they had respect. So, I had to save them."[8]

The Bielski *otriad* had as many as twelve hundred members. Older people, women, and children made up three fourths of the group's population. Most members were escapees from ghettos. They had little knowledge of forest life. If anything, the roles were reversed from those in cities. Craftspeople and tradespeople were more highly regarded now than professors.

After a while, the Bielski group formed its own *shtetl* (village). They lived in *ziemlankas*, bunkers that were two-thirds underground. Their blacksmith and gunsmith got customers from other *otriads* and even nearby villages. A sausage maker gained fame far beyond the area. Tailors, shoemakers, tanners, and barbers also kept busy. The *otriad* accepted food, medicine, or ammunition as pay. All payments went to Tuvia. He distributed them as needed.

Partisan methods were not always entirely honorable. Getting food was a problem. Usually, local peasants contributed, but such contributions were not always voluntary. "A partisan was something between a hero and a robber," said one partisan. "We had to live and we had to deprive the peasants of their meager belongings. These natives were punished by the Germans and by us."[9] If possible, the Bielskis avoided the peasants who had little food. The wealthiest, those with food to spare, were the main targets.

Even though the Bielskis worried mainly about survival, they also attacked. Once Tuvia and a thief named Israel Kesler led a raid on an anti-Semitic gang. They pretended to be anti-Jewish bounty hunters. The gang leader talked about how much he hated Jews. Then one Bielski member said, "I am a Jew too!" They shot the gang leader and his family, then left a sign on the door. "This family was annihilated because it cooperated with the Germans and pursued Jews, signed The Bielski Company."[10] Soon other houses displayed the same message. When villages feared such reprisal, anti-Jewish actions ceased.

In late 1942, the Bielskis sabotaged local harvests. Large estates, under control of the Nazis, saw their crops burned. Partisans stationed themselves to stop anyone who tried to fight those fires.

The camp was never entirely safe. German raids could take place at any time. Members had to be ready to travel through mud and mosquitoes in the summer and through snow and ice in the winter.

Partisan groups worked with the Russians. It appeared to be a matter of time until the Soviet army reached Belorussia. Yet the partisans, particularly Jews, wanted their independence.

Russian troops advanced on Belorussia in June 1944. Jewish partisans helped by destroying roads and bridges that brought German reinforcements. Later, they hunted with Soviets for fleeing Germans. They reached Novogrudok, where the Bielskis once lived, in July. The Bielskis held a victory parade, and Tuvia gave

Members of the Bielski partisan unit pose for a group portrait. The resistance unit, containing nearly twelve hundred members, operated in western Belorussia.

his followers documents. Then the Bielski *otriad*, the largest Jewish partisan group, disbanded.

Faye Lazebnik

"In reality, wherever there was the slightest opportunity, Jews fought back."[11] That was the claim of Faye Lazebnik Schulman. As a teenager, Faye fought as a member of the Molotava partisan brigade.

Lazebnik lived in Lenin, Poland. Soviets claimed Lenin and other eastern Polish towns soon after Germany's 1939 invasion. Two years later, they attacked Soviet-occupied Poland, including Lenin. In July 1942, they massacred Lenin's inhabitants. Lazebnik's parents, sisters, a younger brother, brother-in-law, and sister's children perished.

Only a handful of Lenin residents survived. These included the families of a carpenter, tailor, shoemaker, blacksmith, and printer, and photographer Faye Lazebnik. All had skills the Nazis needed. Yet even their slave-labor existence was uncertain. The Nazis gave Lazebnik a Ukrainian assistant. When that assistant learned necessary photography skills, Faye Lazebnik could be executed.

One day in 1942, a partisan group raided the town. Lazebnik and the few remaining Jews escaped. She went to the partisans' commander. Most partisan groups in Poland sought neither Jews nor women. But this commander knew of Lazebnik's camera skills. He let her stay as photographer and nurse.

Lazebnik took pictures of partisan members and activities. She also tended to wounded fighters. But Faye Lazebnik did much more. She served as a scout and occasional fighter. On a typical trip she might carry a gun, grenade, medicine bag, and camera.

On one trip back to Lenin, Lazebnik received an unexpected "present." A priest gave her a Jewish girl whom he had been hiding. Lazebnik took the girl back to camp. This partisan group, like many others, did not want children. Even so, Lazebnik took care of the girl. A year later, she sent the girl on an airplane to Russia.

As a partisan, Lazebnik encountered some major tragedies. Once she was sent to deliver a message to another partisan group. She and a partner traveled by canoe. When the partner tried to pull the canoe to shore, a mine blew up and killed him. Another time, Lazebnik volunteered to go on a mission. Her commander told her it might be dangerous, but she decided to go anyway. When she returned, she found that her whole camp had been slaughtered.

"We may have been poorly equipped, but our main weapon, personal courage, was in abundant supply," Lazebnik commented. "We fought hard and with surprising success, knowing that surrender meant torture and death. There was no other way to survive. We had to win."[12]

The Magnificent Heroic Struggle

Survival—that was the key. Jews during the Holocaust did what they could to stay alive. If they did not move to save themselves, it was often because they did not want to cause harm to family or friends. When it became clear that no one might be saved, revolt was the only choice. But by then, it was often too late.

The Warsaw Ghetto

Jews thrived in Warsaw during the 1930s. A lively culture made the Polish capital the European Jewish center. Music, film, theater, and newspapers flourished. Writers, economists, political leaders, and rabbis were drawn there from Lithuania, Russia, and the Polish provinces. In 1939, the Jewish population of Warsaw was 375,000—almost 30 percent of the city's total. Five years later, the official Jewish population there would be zero.

Nazi troops attacked Poland with lightning speed in September 1939. Poles put up a gallant fight. But in less than a month, Poland was conquered.

More than three hundred thousand Jews fled Warsaw in the early days of the war. Many of those who remained were the very old and the very young, or women with small children. Most of them were people who could not put up a meaningful resistance. Later, Nazis brought in tens of thousands of other Jewish prisoners from the Polish provinces and neighboring countries.

The conquering Nazis immediately placed restrictions on these Jews. These were the same laws that worked so well in Germany. Jews were identified, then forced to wear the Jewish star. Professionals could no longer practice law or medicine. Nazis marked Jewish stores, warning non-Jews not to shop there. Jews could no longer own radios.

Nazis also reintroduced the ghetto in 1939. During many periods in history, Jews were forced into isolated areas called ghettos. This time, the ghetto situation was particularly severe. Jews could not change their place of residence. They could not use railroads without special permission. They had to register all possessions. For the most part, Jews resigned themselves to these embarrassing rules. They and their ancestors had endured humiliations before. Surely these too would pass.

Germans established a *Judenrat* in each ghetto. These were Jewish councils created to handle daily ghetto affairs but under direct orders of the Nazis. Many Jews considered *Judenrat* members to be Nazi puppets, with no real power to affect or alter Nazi policy.

At first, the ghetto was open. Jews could leave during the day to shop or go to jobs on the outside. Occasionally, a ghetto resident would escape. Vladka Meed related, "I took off my [star-marked] armband and ran away. In a few blocks, I was a Polish girl."[1] But in November 1940, an eleven-foot wall topped with barbed wire and broken glass sealed Warsaw's ghetto. Now those without work passes were trapped inside. The only exits were one-way trips—to cemeteries or death camps.

Ghetto existence was a living hell. More than seven people shared the average room. Bad sanitary conditions caused widespread disease. German regulations allowed Jews "less than 10 percent of the minimum calorie requirements necessary to sustain human life."[2] Any extra food had to be smuggled into the ghetto from the outside. Smugglers charged hefty rates for the simplest foodstuffs.

For Jewish children, death was a plaything. They played at grave digging. Another game they played was gatekeeper. The "Germans" got to beat up on the "Jews."

Even fellow Jews could not be trusted. Some *Judenrat* members did all they could to block Nazi cruelties. Others turned fellow Jews over to the Nazis in order to save themselves and their families. Jewish police patrolled the ghetto. Acting out of fear for their own lives, they were at times crueler and more sadistic than the Nazis. Informers were everywhere. They were ready to tell Nazis of any planned revolt or underground movement. Their only reward was to live another day. If they could no longer give information, they too were killed.

Ghetto residents were victims of forced labor. In addition to the labor camps, residents in the ghettos also worked in factories for the Nazis. In some ghettos the workers did not get paid by the Nazis. However, those ghetto residents who had money hidden away paid poorer people to work for them.

Despite these conditions, there was little thought of revolt or escape. One ghetto newspaper said escapees were traitors for "endangering the existence of our entire ghetto and the lives of their loved ones."[3] In

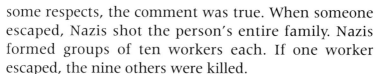

some respects, the comment was true. When someone escaped, Nazis shot the person's entire family. Nazis formed groups of ten workers each. If one worker escaped, the nine others were killed.

Many councils warned that revolt meant certain death for the entire ghetto. With forced labor, there was at least a chance of survival for some. They hoped non-resistance would buy time until Allied troops could liberate them. For most, the only thing nonresistance bought was their death certificates.

"All Jewish Persons . . . Will Be Resettled"

Had the Nazis been patient, they could have starved most Jews to death. Disease, starvation, and Nazi cruelty took eighty-five thousand Jewish lives between September 1939 and July 1942. Twenty thousand people died from typhus alone. But that death rate was too slow for the Nazis. Before 1942, they lacked an efficient way to kill the Jews. In late 1942, death camps opened with the necessary killing mechanism.

Rumors spread in June 1942 that the Nazis planned some kind of raid against the Warsaw ghetto. *Judenrat* leader Adam Czerniakow asked the ghetto commander about the rumors. The Nazi said he knew nothing about them.

A few weeks later, the Nazi leader came back to Czerniakow. He needed the *Judenrat* director's help with the "resettlements" of Warsaw Jews. Czerniakow felt there was little else he could do. The Nazis were holding his wife hostage. He signed an order allowing the deportation. On July 22, a poster appeared throughout

Vladka Meed removed her star-marked armband and escaped the Warsaw ghetto.

the ghetto: "The *Judenrat* has been informed of the following: All Jewish persons living in Warsaw, regardless of age and sex, will be resettled in the East."[4] Thousands of Jews, beginning with the oldest, youngest, and weakest, would be moved away in cattle cars.

On July 23, Czerniakow wrote his last words: "The SS wants me to kill children with my own hands. There is no other way out. . . ."[5] Then he swallowed a cyanide pill and ended his life.

The "resettlements" emptied the ghetto. Its population fell from about 390,000 to 70,000 between July and September of 1942. Those with jobs were most likely to escape deportation. German factory owners took advantage of the Jews' desperation. They demanded money from Jews for the "right" to work without pay at their factories.

At first, Warsaw Jews might have believed stories about "resettlement" in the East. But Nazis claimed the new camps were three days away by train, and the same trains kept returning to Warsaw every day. An Aryan-looking Jew named Aalman Fredrych slipped out of the ghetto. He followed a train to Treblinka and saw the death camp. When he returned to Warsaw, the ghetto knew the truth.

By then, the ghetto looked like a ghost town. Jews could walk the streets only between 5:00 and 7:30 A.M. and 4:00 and 8:00 P.M. Stores could open only during those hours.

The time for self-delusion was over. There could be no denying that Nazis intended to kill all ghetto residents. Chances of survival were slim. Chances of victory were none. But if Jews were going to perish, they could do so with bravery and dignity. If they died, they would take enemy troops with them.

Ghetto residents organized the *Zydowska Organizacja Bojowa* (ZOB), or Jewish Fighting Organization, which was set up with the intent of building resistance. Another similar group, the ZZW (Jewish Fighting Union), followed. The ZOB declared, in a public statement, its members' willingness to "die like human beings."[6]

The resistance needed a leader, and it got one. Mordecai Anielewicz had worked with the underground in the Polish province of Silesia. He returned to Warsaw and built a disciplined fighting unit. First he had to smuggle in weapons. This was no easy task. Polish underground members had little desire to aid what they considered a lost Jewish cause. Arms, when obtainable, were expensive.

The next step was to eliminate subversive units within the ghetto—those who had cooperated with the Nazis. Jewish police commander Jozef Szerynski, according to one diarist, had "aided in the execution of 200,000 Jews."[7] On August 20, 1942, he was shot in the face but survived. Two months later, Jacob Lejkin, Szerynski's replacement, was killed. Another act of vengeance occurred when Yisrael First, a prominent *Judenrat* employee, was killed. Nazi collaborators got the message. It was more dangerous to oppose the Jews than to oppose the Nazis.

ZOB members planned a demonstration for January 22, 1943. A second wave of deportations changed their plans.

"The Jews Have Weapons!"

SS leader and head of the Gestapo Heinrich Himmler visited the ghetto on January 9, 1943. A few days later, he called for more deportations. This time, Mordecai Anielewicz and the ZOB called for armed resistance. "Not a single Jew should go to the railroad cars," he urged.[8]

Nazis entered the ghetto on January 18. At 6:00 A.M., they ordered Jews onto the streets. They were to march to the *Umschlagplatz* (transit point) for deportation to Treblinka, an extermination camp. This appeared to be an easy job.

Suddenly, some of the marchers attacked. They used fists, pistols, and other weapons against the soldiers. Other ghetto residents then fled to prearranged hiding places. German troops went from building to building to catch the renegades. ZOB members began firing at them. One Nazi soldier shouted, "Dear God! The Jews have weapons!"[9]

The first skirmishes were open street battles. These proved costly to the Jews. Too many died. Then they switched to hit-and-run guerrilla tactics. German troops stayed away from attics, cellars, or other places where they might be ambushed. They would not risk their own lives just to take someone else's. By the third day, it was the Jews who were bold and the Germans who were frightened.

Ghetto commander Jürgen Stroop called off the action after the third day. Seven hundred ZOB members had held off two thousand German soldiers. Only 6,500 Jews out of more than 40,000, most of them ill or unlucky, had been taken. Stroop was enraged that "this trash and subhumanity" would not submit peaceably.[10] For the next two months, Germans stopped further deportations. Politics, not surrender, caused this lull. The SS wanted all Jews killed immediately. The *Wehrmacht* (regular German army) wanted them alive. They needed Jewish labor to produce weapons and war supplies. Poles could not replace the Jewish workers. Able-bodied Polish workers were already in labor camps.

Ghetto Jews had no time to worry about these power struggles. They prepared for more action. The

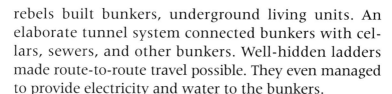

rebels built bunkers, underground living units. An elaborate tunnel system connected bunkers with cellars, sewers, and other bunkers. Well-hidden ladders made route-to-route travel possible. They even managed to provide electricity and water to the bunkers.

The Polish underground could provide only a few weapons, which came mainly from German policemen who were willing to sell them for a high price (which most Jews could not afford). Still, every ZOB member had a revolver. Most also had four or five grenades. ZOB and ZZW forces prepared about two thousand Molotov cocktails. These were homemade bombs of bottles filled with gasoline.

German troops lined up outside the ghetto at 2:00 A.M. on April 19. This time they were prepared for war. The Nazis were going after a military enemy, not defenseless victims.

At 6:00 A.M., they attacked. Jews beat them back with a ferocious response. During the night, they had blockaded the ghetto entrance. While the Nazis dug through furniture and overturned wagons, ghetto residents showered them with gunfire and bombs. Well-placed mines killed dozens of soldiers.

The Nazis had hoped for victory within three days. Instead, the Jews fought them for more than a month. "What has happened has exceeded our dreams," Mordecai Anielewicz wrote on April 23. "Jewish armed resistance and retaliation have become a reality. I have been witness to the magnificent heroic struggle of the Jewish fighters."[11]

Stroop's patience disappeared. Regular troop warfare was producing few results. He called for the ghetto's destruction. "During the first three days of fighting, the Jews had the upper hand," wrote a resistance fighter known as Kajik. "From then on, their onslaught came entirely from the outside, through air attack and artillery. We couldn't resist the bombing, especially their method of setting fire to the ghetto. The whole ghetto was ablaze. All life vanished from the streets and houses."[12] When ghetto residents tried to flee burning buildings, Nazi sharpshooters killed them. Even the bunkers became death traps. Anielewicz wrote that it was almost impossible to light a candle in his bunker. Overcrowding led to a lack of oxygen in the underground room.

The bunker under 18 Mila Street served as the fighters' headquarters. Underground smugglers had built Mila 18, as the bunker was known. ZOB leaders joined them. More than three hundred people—crooks and battle strategists alike—shared the three-block-long shelter.

The Nazis shot poison gas into Mila 18 on May 8. Most inhabitants suffocated. Only a few escaped. Those who fled still had breathed the poison gas. No one from Mila 18 lived to see liberation.

Stroop crowed about his victory. He wrote a seventy-five-page leather-bound report titled *The Warsaw Ghetto Is No More*. His boasts were slightly premature. As late as June, a handful of Jews took potshots at Nazis inside the ghetto.

Some ghetto-dwellers escaped through the sewer system. One wrote, "The lid of the sewer over our head literally opened and a flood of sunlight streamed in. . . . We started to climb out one after another. . . . The streets were crowded with people, and everybody stood still

In the top photo, Commander Jurgen Stroop (second from left) and German soldiers examine the burning Warsaw ghetto. Nazis were shocked by the intensity of Warsaw's ghetto uprising. German soldiers (bottom) round up Jews who participated in the Warsaw ghetto uprising.

and watched, while strange beings, hardly recognizable as humans, crawled out of the sewers."[13]

Fifteen to twenty thousand Jews, hidden by Christians, survived in Warsaw. But Germans knocked down the ghetto walls in September. The ghetto indeed was no more.

Death Camp Escapes

Jews' chances of living through ghetto revolts were slim. Their chances of surviving death camp rebellions were even less. Yet some inmates tried death camp attacks. They had nothing to lose.

Treblinka prisoners learned of the Warsaw ghetto uprising. The revolt, though unsuccessful, gave them inspiration. Four prisoners, led by Warsaw doctor Julian Chorazycki, met nightly to plan a revolt.

The conspirators planned to smuggle weapons into Treblinka. Security guards, if bribed well enough, would ignore the arms sales. One SS lieutenant, Kurt Franz, could not be bought. He saw a wad of Polish *zlotys* in Chorazycki's pocket. Before Franz could ask the doctor where he got the money, Chorazycki ran. He drank poison before Franz could catch him and died without talking.

Plans for a revolt continued. A Jewish locksmith fixed the lock at the camp armory. Unknown to the Nazis, he made copies of the armory key. Jews now had quick access to the camp's weapons. They planned to disarm guards, cut off communications, destroy all death camp equipment, and escape to form a partisan unit.

The rebels planned their revolt for August 2, 1943, at 5:00 P.M. By two o'clock they began distributing arms. At 3:45 P.M. a single gunshot was supposed to be the signal to begin the revolt. However, a half hour earlier an SS man was shot by two prisoners. The rest of the revolters understood this to be the signal. They began; fires, bombs, and shots surprised the soldiers. But the revolters had not been completely ready. Chiel Rajchman recalled, "Our plan was to get out of there and free the penal camp, but we were not able to do it. After a few moments, the Germans started shooting and killing. . . .I was screaming, 'People, save yourselves!' . . . I was one of the last to leave. When I left many were lying on the ground, already dead."[14] About two hundred inmates escaped. Many of those were betrayed by local Poles and turned over to the SS.

Another attempt, at the Sobibór death camp, took place that October. Inmates had heard that the camp was closing. This meant, most likely, that they would soon be killed. Aleksander Pechersky planned the revolt. Jews would kill camp leaders, grab weapons, and escape to the countryside.

The revolt started in the camp tailor shop. The tailor arranged for officers, one at a time, to come to his shop for uniform fittings. When the officer put down his weapons to try on the uniform, a prisoner would grab the gun and shoot him.

One SS official arrived at the shop unexpectedly. He saw a dead comrade, then sounded an alarm. Many prisoners had no idea what was happening. Others tried futile attacks upon the armed Nazi troops. Many rushed toward the field that surrounded the camp. Some of them died in explosions in the heavily mined area. Stanislaw Szmajzner remembered, "I was able to save my life by climbing to freedom over the dead bodies lying on the mines."[15] About sixty prisoners, including Pechersky, survived.

In the death camps, work crews called *Sonderkommandos* were appointed from among the Jewish prisoners. Their function in the camps was to drag the bodies of their fellow Jewish inmates to the crematorium and then scatter their ashes. In October 1944, a revolt

led by three hundred Greek Jews of the *Sonderkommando* in the death camp of Birkenau had been organized.

Young Jewish women of the camp had smuggled explosives and small arms to the *Sonderkommando*. After this the organizers of the revolt were told not to rebel because it could provoke the murder of the entire camp. However, on October 7, prisoners began throwing stones at SS men, as other rebels set fire to a crematorium. At other crematoriums located throughout the camp, prisoners used the few smuggled weapons they had to shoot at guards. At the conclusion of the revolt, one crematorium was burned down, 450 of 650 rebels died, and only a few SS guards were killed or wounded.

Auschwitz, the largest death camp, posed a special problem. It housed political prisoners as well as death camp inmates. The non-Jewish political prisoners had a chance to survive if they did not rebel. To them, every day was a day closer to freedom. To Jews, however, every day was a day closer to a gas chamber.

Jewish prisoners Alfred Wetzler and Walter Rosenberg (Rudolf Vrba) examined the situation. Escape, not revolt, was their answer. If they got word to the outside, others might rescue the Auschwitz prisoners.

Two hours before roll call on April 7, 1944, the young men hid in a woodpile. Fellow prisoners sprinkled the area with gasoline and tobacco so that guard dogs could not sniff them. Wetzler and Rosenberg stayed hidden for three days. Auschwitz officials, figuring they had escaped, withdrew the guards surrounding the camp. Wetzler and Rosenberg made it to the outside. They described the horrors of Auschwitz to anyone who would listen.

10

Whoever Saves a Single Soul

Adolf Hitler boasted that his Third Reich would last a thousand years. It survived only twelve. The Nazi empire crumbled under the weight of its own evil. Allied forces—American and British forces in the West and the Soviet Union in the East—liberated Europe from its German rulers.

Liberation came at different times for different groups. Soviet troops moved into western Belorussia in July 1944. With this conquest, the work of the Bielski *otriad* was done. André and Magda Trocmé heard a rumbling of tanks in September 1944. They waved the French tricolor flag with joy when American forces arrived at Le Chambon. Raoul Wallenberg welcomed Soviet forces into Budapest, Hungary, in January 1945.

The master of ceremonies interrupted a May 1945 performance in a theater in Stockholm, Sweden. "Ladies and Gentlemen," he announced, "just now we have been informed that the Germans have capitulated. . . . Denmark is liberated!"[1]

"You might as well have dropped a bomb in the theater," Danish actor Sam Besekow recalled. "People jumped up from their seats, embracing, rushing the stage and the orchestra, throwing programs into the air. A volcano had erupted. . . . The audience behaved more crazily than the vaudeville company, crying, yelling, weeping, dancing."[2]

Adolf Hitler is believed to have committed suicide on April 30, 1945, in his bunker in Berlin. A few days later, the Soviet army entered Warsaw. Jews found the spot where the Mila 18 bunker had stood. They placed a monument there. It read, "Here on the 8th day of May 1943, Mordecai Anielewicz, the commander of the Warsaw ghetto uprising, together with the staff of the Jewish Fighting Organization and dozens of fighters, fell in the campaign against the Nazi enemy."[3]

Scorned and Praised

What happened to those heroes who risked their lives to save Jews from the Holocaust? Some were praised and some were scorned. Some were scorned and later praised.

André and Magda Trocmé continued to live by their pacifist ideals. André later became the European head of the Fellowship of Reconciliation. He died in 1971. Magda passed away in late 1996.

Early in the morning on January 17, 1945, Russian soldiers entered Budapest and summoned Raoul Wallenberg to Soviet military headquarters. "I'm not

Shortly after the end of the war, sculptor Nathan Rapaport created this monument of the Warsaw resistance movement. It was built on the site of the former Warsaw ghetto.

sure whether I'm their guest or their prisoner," he told a friend when he left.[4] He was never seen in the free world again. The Soviet government claimed that he died in a Russian prison in 1947, but he was reported alive as late as 1974. Despite his reported imprisonment, Wallenberg was greatly praised in the West for his rescue work. The United States proclaimed him an honorary American citizen in 1981.

Two other diplomats met rejection at home. Aristides de Sousa Mendes was removed from the diplomatic corps when he returned to Portugal. The formerly wealthy Mendes also lost his social connections. He died penniless in 1954. His family sought to save his good name. In 1987, they succeeded. Sousa Mendes received a posthumous Order of Liberty from the Portuguese government. In 1988, he was restored to full diplomatic rank.

Sempo Sugihara likewise lost his position when he returned to Tokyo. He, too, died in disgrace. Later, however, the Japanese government dedicated the "Hill of Humanity" in Yastu to him.

Nazis failed to identify Georg Ferdinand Duckwitz as the man who tipped off Danes to German plans. Duckwitz survived the war at his post and remained a diplomat afterward. Danes warmly greeted him after the war as West Germany's ambassador to Denmark.

Niels Bohr went to England, then to the United States. He played a major role in the development of the atomic bomb. Bohr later returned to Denmark.

Oskar Schindler escaped to Western Europe after the war, then spent some time in Argentina. He tried a number of business ventures. All failed. By the end of his life, he was living off the generosity of those he had saved. Germans turned their backs on him, but Jews gave him a hero's welcome when he visited Tel Aviv,

Israel, in 1961. Schindler died in 1974. More than four hundred Jews and their families attended his funeral.

Many Dutch rescuers became disillusioned after the war. They saw the Dutch government appointing known Nazi collaborators to powerful positions. Aart and Johtje Vos were among those disappointed heroes. They left the Netherlands and moved to the United States. The Dutch government, however, later made the Frank hiding place at 263 Prinsengracht a national monument.

Eva Cohn's family survived the war intact. Afterward, they tried to thank the police commander who had helped them. "We found that he did not survive the war," Eva said. "He was shipped to the Russian front. That was almost always a death sentence." The mysterious Russian-speaking man who had helped her father at the police station disappeared. "He was a spy," she said. "This much we know."[5] Eva's family returned to Antwerp, Belgium, after the war. She married a man named Shane and moved to Chicago.

The Bielskis did not enjoy good fortune. The Red Army drafted Asael. He died in battle in Germany. Tuvia and Zus went to Israel and joined the army there. Both went with their families to Brooklyn, New York, in the 1950s and worked in the trucking business. Their partisan exploits were largely ignored.

Faye Lazebnik reunited with her brother Moshe after the war. She also found an old friend from Lenin, Moshe Schulman. He, too, had been an active partisan member. Lazebnik and Schulman married soon afterward. They moved to Canada in 1948.

Angelo Giuseppe Roncalli received the highest honor the Catholic Church could bestow. Fellow cardinals elected him pope in 1958. As Pope John XXIII, he instituted church reforms and called for unity among all Christians.

The United States Holocaust Memorial Museum in Washington, D.C., displays the horrors of the Holocaust and honors many of the era's heroes.

Yad Vashem

Six million European Jews died at the hands of the Nazis. Not long after the war, surviving Jews had a homeland. In 1948, the nation of Israel was created from the Middle Eastern land of Palestine. Jews flocked to the country their ancestors had left two thousand years earlier.

The Israeli government swore that the Holocaust, and its heroes, would not be forgotten. It created the Yad Vashem Holocaust Martyrs and Heroes Memorial Authority in 1953. In 1963, it established a museum to honor non-Jews for their heroism during the Holocaust. Each year, ceremonies honor these "righteous Gentiles." Honorees have their deeds recounted at the ceremony. They receive a plaque bearing their name and nationality. The government plants a carob tree in their name on the Avenue of the Righteous. More than sixteen thousand trees have been planted.

Many honorees did not wish to discuss their accomplishments. "At first we were reluctant [to talk about our experiences]," Johtje Vos said. "But a rabbi told me, 'You must talk about it. You have a responsibility. You're the last generation who saw it, and you have no right to be modest about it.'"[6] Another honoree, Ivan Beltrami, accepted a medal from Yad Vashem in 1984. He told the director that he didn't think he really deserved the honor. The director assured him that he did, and added, "All the righteous say the same thing."[7]

"It Is As If He Saved the Whole World"

Holocaust heroes have received medals and prizes for their activities. For many, the greatest rewards were those that could not be measured.

Kate Lipner had Thanksgiving guests in 1996. These were no ordinary visitors. After World War II, Kate Rossi returned the children in her care to their mother. Then she married an American soldier named Lipner and moved to Chicago in 1946. Fifty years later, two grown children of the children she had saved came to visit her. These young adults would never have been born if Kate had not saved their parents.

She showed them her Yad Vashem medal. The inscription described her and thousands of other heroes as well. The medal read: "Whoever saves a single soul, it is as if he saved the whole world."

Chronology

1918

Germany loses World War I.

1923

Adolf Hitler's Beer Hall *Putsch*, an attempt to take over the German government, fails.

1925

Mein Kampf, Hitler's autobiography detailing his hatred of Jews, is published.

1933

Hitler becomes chancellor of Germany and immediately issues laws depriving Jews of their rights.

1935

Nuremberg Laws take away Jews' German citizenship.

July 1938

Évian Conference, representing thirty-two nations, fails to solve Jewish refugee problems.

November 9–10, 1938

Nazis destroy thousands of Jewish synagogues and businesses in a night of destruction known as *Kristallnacht* ("Night of Broken Glass").

May 1939

S.S. *St. Louis*, filled with Jewish refugees, is turned back at the Havana, Cuba, harbor and forced to return to Europe. Most of its passengers would die in the Holocaust.

September 1, 1939

Germany invades Poland; World War II begins.

July 1940

Sempo Sugihara signs thousands of travel visas, saving Jews in Kovno, Lithuania.

November 1940

Nazis enclose Warsaw ghetto behind an eleven-foot wall.

September 1941
> German government requires all Jews to wear the six-pointed Star of David on their clothing.

January 1942
> Wannsee Conference of Nazi leaders discusses the "final solution," the murder of all Europe's Jews.

July 1942
> Anne Frank and her family go into hiding; Nazis deport thousands of Jews from Warsaw ghetto.

January 1943
> Warsaw ghetto Jews fight back, foiling a second mass deportation.

April 1943
> Jews fight bravely, but ultimately unsuccessfully, in Warsaw ghetto uprising.

September 1943
> Georg Ferdinand Duckwitz tells Danish political leaders of upcoming deportation of Jews. Within a month, almost all of Denmark's Jews are evacuated safely to Sweden.

1944
> United States government creates the War Refugee Board, which helps fund Raoul Wallenberg's rescue efforts in Budapest, Hungary.

August 1944
> Nazis capture Anne Frank, her family, and those hiding with them.

January 1945
> Soviet troops capture Raoul Wallenberg. He is believed to have later died in a Russian prison.

April 30, 1945
> Adolf Hitler commits suicide.

May 7, 1945
> Germany surrenders unconditionally to Allies.

1948
> The Jewish nation of Israel is created.

Chapter Notes

Chapter 1. It Would Have Been the End

1. Author's interview with Kate (Rossi) Lipner, December 1, 1996.

Chapter 2. This Craziness

1. Michael R. Marrus, *The Holocaust in History* (Hanover, N.H.: University Press of New England, 1987), p. 109.

2. William L. Shirer, *The Rise and Fall of the Third Reich* (New York: Simon & Schuster, 1960), p. 25.

3. Ibid., p. 26.

4. Albert Speer, *Inside the Third Reich*, trans. Richard and Clara Winston (New York: Collier Books, 1981), p. 17.

5. Eva Fogelman, *Conscience and Courage: Rescuers of Jews During the Holocaust* (New York: Doubleday, 1994), p. 24.

6. Harpo Marx with Rowland Barber, *Harpo Speaks!* (New York: Limelight Editions, 1985), p. 301.

7. Author's interview with Eva (Cohn) Shane, December 20, 1996.

8. Michael Berenbaum, *The World Must Know: The History of the Holocaust as Told in the United States Holocaust Memorial Museum* (Boston: Little, Brown and Company, 1993), p. 41.

9. Ibid., p. 54.

10. Hans Rothfels, *The German Opposition to Hitler* (Chicago: Henry Regnery and Company, 1962), p. 31.

11. *The Holocaust in Memory of Millions*, Discovery Communications, Inc., 1993.

12. Helen Fein, *Accounting for Genocide: National Responses and Jewish Victimization During the Holocaust* (New York: The Free Press, 1979), p. 156.

13. Klaus D. Fischer, *Nazi Germany: A New History* (New York: Continuum, 1995), p. 339.

14. Conference, Harold Washington Library, Chicago, November 24, 1996.

15. Author's interview with Eva (Cohn) Shane, December 20, 1996.

16. Permanent exhibit, United States Holocaust Memorial Museum, Washington, D.C.

Chapter 3. The Right Thing to Do

1. Gay Block and Malka Drucker, *Rescuers: Portraits of Moral Courage in the Holocaust* (New York: Holmes and Meier Publishers, 1992), p. 156.

2. Lecture, Harold Washington Library, Chicago, November 12, 1996.

3. Block and Drucker, pp. 36–37.

4. Helen Fein, *Accounting for Genocide: National Responses and Jewish Victimization During the Holocaust* (New York: The Free Press, 1979), p. 156.

5. Ibid.

6. Rhoda G. Lewin, ed., *Witnesses to the Holocaust: An Oral History* (Boston: Twayne Publishers, 1990), p. 151.

7. Ibid., p. 147.

8. Author's interview with Kate (Rossi) Lipner, December 1, 1996.

9. Block and Drucker, p. 63.

10. "Rescuers of the Holocaust: Portraits by Gay Block," exhibit at Harold Washington Library, Chicago, November 24, 1996.

11. Carol Rittner and Sondra Myers, eds., *The Courage to Care: Rescuers of Jews During the Holocaust* (New York: New York University Press, 1986), p. 70.

12. Author's interview with Kate (Rossi) Lipner, December 1, 1996.

13. Block and Drucker, p. 82.

14. Milton Meltzer, *Rescue: The Story of How Gentiles Saved Jews in the Holocaust* (New York: HarperTrophy, 1988), p. 138.

15. Ibid., p. 139.

16. Miep Gies with Alison Leslie Gold, *Anne Frank Remembered: The Story of the Woman Who Helped to Hide the Frank Family* (New York: Simon & Schuster, 1987), p. 129.

17. Eva Fogelman, *Conscience and Courage: Rescuers of Jews During the Holocaust* (New York: Doubleday, 1994), p. 67.

18. Author's interview with Eva (Cohn) Shane, December 20, 1996.

19. Ibid.

20. Ibid.

21. Ibid.

22. Ibid.

23. Ibid.

24. Fogelman, p. 54.

25. Meltzer, p. 58.

26. Eric Silver, *The Book of the Just: The Unsung Heroes Who Rescued Jews from Hitler* (New York: Grove Press, 1992), p. 148.

27. Lewin, p. 140.

28. Elinor J. Brecher, *Schindler's Legacy: True Stories of the List Survivors* (New York: Dutton Books, 1994), p. xxxi.

29. Ibid., p. xxxii.

Chapter 4. Christians Must Not Forget

1. Michael Berenbaum, *The World Must Know: The History of the Holocaust as Told in the United States Holocaust Memorial Museum* (Boston: Little, Brown and Company, 1993), p. 160.

2. Permanent exhibit, United States Holocaust Memorial Museum, Washington, D.C.

3. Berenbaum, p. 169.

4. Martin Gilbert, *Auschwitz and the Allies* (New York: Holt, Rinehart and Winston, 1981), p. 123.

5. Alexander Ramati, *The Assisi Underground: The Priests Who Rescued Jews* (New York: Stein and Day, 1978), p. 155.

6. Ibid., p. 166.

7. Ibid., p. 178.

8. Fernande Leboucher, *Incredible Mission* (Garden City, N.Y.: Doubleday and Company, 1969), p. 51.

9. Ibid., p. 62.

10. Ibid., p. 118.

Chapter 5. Leave These People Alone

1. Eric Silver, *The Book of the Just: The Unsung Heroes Who Rescued Jews from Hitler* (New York: Grove Press, 1992), p. 53.

2. Ibid., p. 57.

3. Permanent exhibit, United States Holocaust Memorial Museum, Washington, D.C.

4. Michael Berenbaum, *The World Must Know: The History of the Holocaust as Told in the United States Holocaust Memorial Museum* (Boston: Little, Brown and Company, 1993), p. 166.

5. Silver, p. 35.

6. Berenbaum, p. 145.

7. *Safe Haven*, Public Broadcasting Service, 1989.

8. *Missing Hero*, BBC-TV, 1980.

9. John Bierman, *Righteous Gentile: The Story of Raoul Wallenberg, Missing Hero of the Holocaust* (New York: The Viking Press, 1981), p. 38.

10. Raoul Wallenberg, *Letters and Dispatches, 1924–1944: Raoul Wallenberg* (New York: Arcade Publishing, 1995), p. 235.

11. Bierman, pp. 81–82.

12. Ibid., p. 82.

Chapter 6. Danes Helping Fellow Danes

1. Helen Fein, *Accounting for Genocide: National Responses and Jewish Victimization During the Holocaust* (New York: The Free Press, 1979), p. 66.

2. Ibid., p. 192.

3. Ibid.

4. Ib Melchior and Frank Brandenburg, *Quest: Searching for Germany's Nazi Past: A Young Man's Story* (Novato, Calif.: Presidio Press, 1990), pp. 193–194.

5. Harold Flender, *Rescue in Denmark* (New York: Holocaust Library, 1963), p. 31.

6. Eric Silver, *The Book of the Just: The Unsung Heroes Who Rescued Jews from Hitler* (New York: Grove Press, 1992), p. 42.

7. Leo Goldberger, ed., *The Rescue of the Danish Jews: Moral Courage Under Stress* (New York: New York University Press, 1987), p. 82.

8. Flender, p. 15.

9. Goldberger, pp. 6–7.

10. Ibid., p. 51.

11. Ibid., p. 77.

12. Milton Meltzer, *Rescue: The Story of How Gentiles Saved Jews in the Holocaust* (New York: HarperTrophy, 1988), p. 98.

13. Carol Rittner and Sondra Myers, eds., *The Courage to Care: Rescuers of Jews During the Holocaust* (New York: New York University Press, 1986), p. 89.

14. *The Holocaust in Memory of Millions*, Discovery Communications, Inc., 1973.

Chapter 7. Bear Witness to This Terrible Nightmare

1. *The Holocaust in Memory of Millions,* Discovery Communications, Inc., 1973.

2. Hermann Langbein, *Against All Hope: Resistance in the Nazi Concentration Camps 1938–1945* (New York: Paragon House, 1994), p. 257.

3. Michael Berenbaum, *The World Must Know: The History of the Holocaust as Told in the United States Holocaust Memorial Museum* (Boston: Little, Brown and Company, 1993), p. 92.

4. Helen Fein, *Accounting for Genocide: National Responses and Jewish Victimization During the Holocaust* (New York: The Free Press, 1979), p. 213.

5. Ibid., p. 221.

6. Ibid., p. 228.

7. Laurel Holliday, *Children in the Holocaust and World War II: Their Secret Diaries* (New York: Washington Square Press, 1995), p. 241.

8. Ibid., p. 239.

9. "Legacy of Life," *Nightline,* ABC-TV, September 9, 1996.

10. Ibid.

11. Ibid.

12. Ibid.

13. Eva Fogelman, *Conscience and Courage: Rescuers of Jews During the Holocaust* (New York: Doubleday, 1994), p. 30.

14. Michael R. Marrus, *The Holocaust in History* (Hanover, N.H.: University Press of New England, 1987), pp. 108–109.

15. Anne Frank, *The Diary of a Young Girl: The Definitive Edition,* ed. Otto H. Frank and Mirjam Pressler, trans. Susan Massolty (New York: Anchor Books/Doubleday, 1995), p. 6.

16. Anne Frank, *The Diary of a Young Girl* (New York: Doubleday, 1967), p. 26.

17. Ibid., p. 66.

18. Ibid., p. 125.

19. Ibid., p. 139.

20. Ibid., p. 287.

Chapter 8. Stood Up and Fought Like Lions

1. Rhoda G. Lewin, ed., *Witnesses to the Holocaust: An Oral History* (Boston: Twayne Publishers 1990), p. 134.

2. Ibid., p. 136.

3. Ibid., p. 168.

4. Michael Berenbaum, *The World Must Know: The History of the Holocaust as Told in the United States Holocaust Memorial Museum* (Boston: Little, Brown and Company, 1993), p. 178.

5. Faye Schulman, *A Partisan's Memoir: Women of the Holocaust* (Toronto: Second Story Press, 1995), p. 100.

6. Nechama Tec, *Defiance: The Bielski Partisans* (New York: Oxford University Press, 1993), pp. 3–4.

7. Ibid., p. 8.

8. Ibid., p. 48.

9. Ibid., p. 73.

10. Ibid., p. 78.

11. Schulman, p. 10.

12. Ibid., p. 166.

Chapter 9. The Magnificent Heroic Struggle

1. *The Holocaust in Memory of Millions*, Discovery Communications, Inc., 1973.

2. Helen Fein, *Accounting for Genocide: National Responses and Jewish Victimization During the Holocaust* (New York: The Free Press, 1979), p. 210.

3. Michael R. Marrus, *The Holocaust in History* (Hanover, N.H.: University Press of New England, 1987), p. 133.

4. Israel Gutman, *Resistance: The Warsaw Ghetto Uprising* (Boston: Houghton Mifflin Company, 1994), p. 134.

5. Gail B. Stewart, *Life in the Warsaw Ghetto* (San Diego: Lucent Books, 1995), p. 92.

6. Gutman, p. xviii.

7. Ibid.

8. Permanent exhibit, United States Holocaust Memorial Museum, Washington, D.C.

9. Stewart, p. 99.

10. William L. Shirer, *The Rise and Fall of the Third Reich* (New York: Simon & Schuster, 1960), p. 976.

11. Gutman, p. xx.

12. Claude Lanzmann, *Shoah: An Oral History of the Holocaust* (New York: Pantheon Books, 1988), p. 197.

13. Gutman, p. xx.

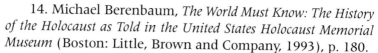

14. Michael Berenbaum, *The World Must Know: The History of the Holocaust as Told in the United States Holocaust Memorial Museum* (Boston: Little, Brown and Company, 1993), p. 180.

15. Hermann Langbein, *Against All Hope: Resistance in the Nazi Concentration Camps, 1938–1945* (New York: Paragon House, 1994), p. 300.

Chapter 10. Whoever Saves a Single Soul

1. Leo Goldberger, ed., *The Rescue of the Danish Jews: Moral Courage Under Stress* (New York: New York University Press, 1987), p. 138.

2. Ibid.

3. Israel Gutman, *Resistance: The Warsaw Ghetto Uprising* (Boston: Houghton Mifflin Company, 1994), p. 259.

4. Sharon Linnéa, *Raoul Wallenberg: The Man Who Stopped Death* (Philadelphia: The Jewish Publication Society, 1993), p. 138.

5. Author's interview with Eva (Cohn) Shane, December 20, 1996.

6. Gay Block and Malka Drucker, *Rescuers: Portraits of Moral Courage in the Holocaust* (New York: Holmes and Meier Publishers, 1992), p. 83

7. Ibid., p. 126.

Further Reading

Barnouw, David, and Gerrold van der Stroom, eds. *The Diary of Anne Frank: The Critical Edition.* New York: Doubleday, 1989.

Bauer, Yehuda. *A History of the Holocaust.* New York: Franklin Watts, 1982.

Berenbaum, Michael. *The World Must Know: The History of the Holocaust as Told in the United States Holocaust Memorial Museum.* Boston: Little, Brown and Company, 1993.

Bierman, John. *Righteous Gentile: The Story of Raoul Wallenberg, Missing Hero of the Holocaust.* New York: Viking Press, 1981.

Brecher, Elinor J. *Schindler's Legacy: True Stories of the List Survivors.* New York: Dutton Books, 1994.

Fischer, Klaus P. *Nazi Germany: A New History.* New York: Continuum, 1995.

Flender, Harold. *Rescue in Denmark.* New York: Simon & Schuster, 1963.

Fogelman, Eva. *Conscience and Courage: Rescuers of the Jews During the Holocaust.* New York: Doubleday, 1994.

Frank, Anne. *Anne Frank: The Diary of a Young Girl.* New York: Doubleday, 1967.

Gies, Miep, with Alison Leslie Gold. *Anne Frank Remembered: The Story of the Woman Who Helped to Hide the Frank Family.* New York: Simon & Schuster, 1987.

Gilbert, Martin. *Auschwitz and the Allies.* New York: Holt, Rinehart and Winston, 1981.

Gutman, Israel. *Resistance: The Warsaw Ghetto Uprising.* Boston: Houghton Mifflin Company, 1994.

Holliday, Laurel. *Children in the Holocaust and World War II: Their Secret Diaries.* New York: Washington Square Press, 1995.

Langbein, Hermann. *Against All Hope: Resistance in the Nazi Concentration Camps 1938–1945.* New York: Paragon House, 1994.

Lanzmann, Claude. *Shoah: An Oral History of the Holocaust.* New York: Pantheon Books, 1985.

Leboucher, Fernande. *Incredible Mission.* Garden City, New York: Doubleday, 1969.

Lewin, Rhoda G., ed. *Witnesses to the Holocaust: An Oral History.* Boston: Twayne Publishers, 1990.

Linnéa, Sharon. *Raoul Wallenberg: The Man Who Stopped Death.* Philadelphia: The Jewish Publication Society, 1993.

Melchior, Ib, and Frank Brandenburg. *Quest: Searching for Germany's Nazi Past: A Young Man's Story.* Novato, Calif.: Presidio Press, 1990.

Meltzer, Milton. *Rescue: The Story of How Gentiles Saved Jews in the Holocaust.* New York: HarperTrophy, 1988.

Pilch, Judah. *The Jewish Catastrophe in Europe.* New York: American Association for Jewish Education, 1988.

Ramati, Alexander. *The Assisi Underground: The Priests Who Rescued Jews.* New York: Stein and Day, 1978.

Ringelblum, Emmanuel. *Notes from the Warsaw Ghetto: The Journal of Emmanuel Ringelblum.* Edited and translated by Jacob Sloan. New York: McGraw-Hill, 1958.

Rittner, Carol, and Sondra Myers, eds. *The Courage to Care: Rescuers of Jews During the Holocaust.* New York: New York University Press, 1981.

Schulman, Faye, with Sarah Silberstein Swartz. *A Partisan's Memoir: Women of the Holocaust.* Toronto: Second Story Press, 1995.

Silver, Eric. *The Book of the Just: The Unsung Heroes Who Rescued Jews from Hitler.* New York: Grove Press, 1992.

Stewart, Gail B. *Life in the Warsaw Ghetto.* San Diego: Lucent Books, Inc., 1995.

Tec, Nechama. *Defiance: The Bielski Partisans.* New York: Oxford University Press, 1993.

Volavkova, Hana, ed. *I Never Saw Another Butterfly: Children's Drawings and Poems from Terezin Concentration Camp, 1942–1944.* New York: Pantheon Books, 1993.

Wallenberg, Raoul. *Letters and Dispatches, 1942–1944: Raoul Wallenberg.* Translated by Kjersti Board. New York: Arcade Publishing, 1987.

Index